DON'T LOSE YOUR
TEMPER
WHEN YOUR *child* DOES

A guide to dealing with **angry** children

DR. PAUL SEIDEL

Want to read more exciting stories for FREE?

Join my **V.I.P** List now!

I regularly GIVEAWAY FREE books and SPECIAL DISCOUNTS!

Join my mailing list and be one of thousands we already receiving FREEBIES!

Join by visiting this site:

paulseidel@ravenspress.com

Or Scan this QR Code from your smartphone to go the website directly

RAVENS PRESS

ISBN-13: 978-1519427717

ISBN-10: 1519427719

paulseidel@ravenspress.com

Table of Contents

Introduction

How do you handle your kids' constant temper tantrums? Do you get frustrated, mystified and end up being angry yourself? Do you panic and rush in to solve your child's problem immediately or do you get caught up in a power struggles? Don't you just wish you could stay composed and rational through all your young child's outbursts of anger?

Dealing with your kids' fits of anger is one of the many challenges and stressful situations you will face as a parent and sometimes you might be unsure if you're doing the right thing. The good news is that you learn as you go. Besides slipping into a fight with your kids, there are realistic and effective ways you can do to triumph over this challenge. Your kids' constant temper flare-ups doesn't mean you're a failure as a parent, it just means that something needs changing.

When confronted with a child's angry behavior, it is important not to take it as a personal attack on you. Your best defense is to understand the circumstances that cause your child to blow a fuse and to prepare yourself for such situations. It pays to have compassion even though you feel like you're at your wits end.

Triggers are different in every child. Sometimes it may need a little hard work to discover the events, thoughts and feelings that precede your kid's anger. By being able to identify and address this anger, you can better help them cope with challenges. You can prevent serious problems that develop if kids don't learn to express their anger in healthy ways.

In this book, we will explore several factors that usually stir up anger in kids, strategies you can use to deal with their angry outbursts and ways you can guide their expressions of anger.

We will also look at different temperament types that can give you helpful insights into what makes your child tick. By taking into consideration that your child's behavior is a result of both his natural inclination and his environment, you can find ways of teaching your kids how to control angry impulses and enhance his overall well-being without changing who he is.

Chapter 1:

Uncovering the Causes of Anger in Kids

Dealing with your children's anger can be puzzling and exhausting. Some parents are filled with embarrassment when their kids display unsettling anger outbursts often for no apparent reason. Yet, there certainly are reasons.

Most of the time, your kids' angry and aggressive behavior push your own angry button, but that's okay because it compels you to fix the problem. You want your kids' behavior corrected and you don't want how it triggers angry feelings in you.

Instead of lashing out at your kids and give in to power struggle, it is important to operate from a place of understanding. This not only increases your tolerance but more importantly, it enables you to teach your kids to master this powerful and complex emotion.

Awareness is the first step to understanding why your kids lose it. One of the biggest mistakes you can make when dealing with a child's angry behavior is creating solutions without understanding the root cause. By having a clear picture of the causes of angry impulses in kids, you can protect them from violent outbursts and help them get a grip of their anger. You can take these behaviors as good opportunities to help your kids learn about self-control.

It is important to remember that anger is not the same thing as aggression. Anger is a feeling, while aggression is a behavior. Feeling angry is okay, hurting another person or destroying property is not. Your goal is not to destroy or repress anger in your kids or in yourself but to manage it in healthy and appropriate ways.

The thing to realize is that anger is a universal reaction to pain. It is normal for children to have episodes of angry outbursts and fighting with other children. Unable to understand and verbalize their frustration in certain situations, kids act out in anger. It can be triggered by loneliness, anxiety, embarrassment and hurt.

To prevent serious problems that develop if children do not learn how to control their angry impulses, you have to get a clear picture of the full range of factors that influence your child's temperamental behavior

Physical discomfort

First, you need to find out if there are biological factors contributing to your child's outbursts. Maybe your child is allergic to dust, pollen or some food and cause him much discomfort. Maybe some ear infection is causing him pain or maybe he finds it difficult to fall asleep or stay asleep throughout the night. Your moods can change too when you're sick.

Life challenges

After ruling out biological factors, figure out other life stressors that may be triggering your kids' anger. Is your child expected to perform beyond his capabilities? Does he feel frustrated because of low academic performance? Identify unsolved problems and lacking skills that cause your child to lose control. Many of the kids who exhibit angry behavior are simply lacking the skills to do the tasks demanded of them. Find out why your child is not doing well on an activity. Knowing your kids, their skills, the demands being put on them allow you to give the kind of support they need to cope with stressful situations.

Parental actions

Some kids have anger problems as a result of modeling after a parent's excessive expression of anger. Are you unconsciously transmitting anger to your child? Are you overly critical or overprotective? You need be aware of your own behavior that may be harming your child's sense of self worth.

Marital discord

When parents fight, they spill over negative emotions to their children. Witnessing bitter and ongoing conflict between parents compounds children's anger and can destroy children's internal unity and security.

Peer Rejection

Anger can result from rejection by peers. Children crave acceptance to develop a healthy self-esteem. You need to be aware of the many ways this rejection can manifest on your child including isolation, hostility toward others and social anxiety.

Temperament

Your child's challenging behavior may be rooted to his natural disposi-
tions and tendencies. You have to be aware of your child's temperament and respect his uniqueness.

Failure to identify and address the cause of anger has serious consequences to your child's mental and emotional health and his relationships with other people. By expressing interest in your kids' activities
and being responsive to anger-triggering situations, it will be easier to
find out what they feel and work through their feelings.

A child finds security from his strong attachments to parents, friends
and relatives. It is important to pay attention to children when they are
looking for love and affection. You should be motivated by the need to
protect and to reach out. Anger in children is often a cry for love and
understanding.

The key takeaway? Take your kids' angry outbursts as a signal to fix
the cause. You'd be surprised at how delightful your kids can be to be
around.

Chapter 2:
Understanding Child's Development

Areas of Child Development

The study of child development is divided into three main areas: biological or physical, cognitive or intellectual, and psychological or social-emotional development. Let's discuss these one by one.

Physical development

Physical development refers to the changes that occur in the body. It is characterized as stable and sequential. While physical changes are understood to be a result of biological processes, the environment also plays a significant role in optimizing development. For example, muscle development will not be enhanced without proper nutrition and motor development will not be optimal without the presence of toys, for example.

Categories of physical development

Gross-motor development – refers to the skills developed by children which involves the muscles in the legs and arms. Examples of skills under this category are riding a bike, skipping, and running.

Fine-motor development – refers to the skills developed by children, and involves the small muscles in the hands and fingers. Example of skills under this category are holding, grasping, drawing, and cutting.

Cognitive development

Cognitive development revolves around the changes children manifest in terms of learning, reasoning, thoughts, language, and imagination. An example of a skill development as a result of cognitive development involves the proper identification of different colors.

Social-emotional development

Social-emotional development is comprised of two areas that are interrelated: social development involves learning how to relate to others while emotional development focuses on feelings and the expression of these feelings. An example of social-emotional development is the development of pride, humor, friendship, interest, and pleasure.

The three areas of development are interdependent. How one area develops affects the two others. For example, without fine-motor skills, a child will not be able to write. Without cognitive development, a child will not know what to write; and without social-emotional development, a child will not know how to express his thoughts in writing.

Principles of Child Development

We know that every child is unique. In fact, every individual — young and old — is unique. But when it comes to development, there are basic patterns which make all of us the same. Hence, child development is considered universal, sequential, and predictable.

The cephalocaudal principle

This principle believes that development starts from the head down to the toes. It presupposes that a child gains control of his head first, then his arms, then his legs. On the head, the child also learns face movements in two months following his birth. After a few months, a child learns how to lift himself using their arms. In 6 to 12 months, the child learns how to crawl, to walk, or to stand.

The proximodistal principle

This principle involves the belief that development starts from the center of the body going outwards. This principle is rooted with the belief that the spinal cord develops before the other parts of the body. Hence, a child's arms and legs develops first before his fingers and toes.

The principle of maturation

The sequence of development involving biological changes is called maturation. The concept of maturation is believed to be highly influenced by the development in the nervous system and primarily the brain. In addition, the role of environment in creating an atmosphere that encourages developmental milestones also affects maturation.

In addition to biological change as an influencer in maturation, developmental milestones cannot be attained until the different parts of the body mature. For example, the brain of a one-year-old baby is not matured enough in order for him to understand words. A two-year-old child's brain is not mature enough in order to verbalize complex ideas. These examples show that development in the brain occurs from simple tasks to more complex tasks.

On the other hand, physical development starts from the development of general skills before specific skills. For example, a child will simply start to grasp toys using his hands. Later on, he will be able to pick toys using his fingers.

Finally, one thing that you need to understand about the principle of child development is "rate of development." This is defined as the pace at which children attain milestones in development. It is common to see children of the same age develop differently. More evident in the classroom, children who start on the same grade level may take different times to finish their assignments or their education in general.

Unless developmental problems are imminent, the rate at which children develop should be considered normal. No development is fast enough that it can be accelerated. Even those with a genius mind take time before they begin to show their exceptional mental capabilities.

Chapter 3:
The Major Child Development Theorists

Sigmund Freud (1856 – 1939)

Theoretical approach: psychodynamic

Freud's psychodynamic theory presupposes that behavior is influenced or controlled by a child's unconscious urges. The three levels of consciousness we know are included in this approach namely, the id, the ego, and the superego.

Maria Montessori (1870 – 1952)

Theoretical approach: Montessori learning

Montessori is one approach to education today. This pedagogical approach was offered by Montessori in response to her belief that children develop (or learn) by being exposed to sensory information and by being given the chance to pursue their own interests.

Arnold Gesell (1880 – 1961)

Theoretical approach: maturation

Gesell's theory upholds the principles that growth and development happens in orderly stages and a linear and progressive sequence. The main factor affecting maturation is the child's genetic makeup or heredity.

Jean Piaget (1896 – 4980) and Lev Vygotsky (1896 – 1934)

Theoretical approach: psychosocial

Piaget and Vygotsky are contemporaries who believe that personality involves eight stages that occurs in a person's lifetime. The pillars of development are family, friends, and culture.

Erik Erikson (1902 – 1994)

Theoretical approach: cognitive

Sometime later after Piaget and Vygotsky focused on the psycho-social correlates of development, Erikson came up with his theory that focuses on cognitive development. His approach offers that the changes in the way children think is influenced by active learning. Hence, changes occur at a qualitative rate among children.

John Watson (1878 – 1958), B.F. Skinner (1904 – 1990), and Albert Bandura (1925)

Theoretical approach: behaviorist

Although they lived at different times, the three theorists above believed that development is a sequence of conditioned behaviors. This approach is the first of its kind to focus on environment as the primary influencer of development. The theory focuses on observable behavior to indicate gradual and continuous learning.

Urie Bronfenbrenner (1917 – 2005)

Theoretical approach: ecological

After earlier theorists focused on the influence of heredity and environment as influencers in child development, Bronfenbrenner came up with his own theory that takes into account nature and nurture as two interwoven factors in child development. He recognized that a child is in the middle of multiple factors that influence his development.

Noam Chomsky (1928 – present)

Theoretical approach: information processing theory

Hailed as the father of modern linguistics, Chomsky, who is also a cognitive scientist, proposed a theory saying that children have an innate learning ability that is characterized by information processing skills. This ability, he says, is the primary influencer that allows children to follow a certain structure of development.

Robert Cole (1929 – present)

Theoretical approach: moral development

Cole's theory emphasizes the role of the parent or the primary caregiver in his theory. He says that in for children to adopt moral learning, he needs to be exposed to moral upbringing and that the primary caregivers and parents should set a good example.

All of the theories mentioned above have their own merits. In fact, there are other theories not included in the list but are included in this book. Since these are all theories, you are encouraged to take an eclectic approach when it comes to understanding child development. No theory is wrong, and no theory is absolutely right. What's important is the insight that we bring into the different behaviors and skills manifested by children as they grow, and what we do about these insights.

Chapter 4:

Personality Development of Children

In order to better understand why children develop certain character-istics like anger temperament, we should look at

Erik Erikson's Psychosocial Theory.

Erik Erikson: The Psychosocial Theory

Erikson's interest in child development did not manifest until he met Anna Freud, the daughter of Sigmund Freud. After going through psy-choanalysis, Erikson decided to become an analyst himself. He then went to the Vienna Psychoanalytic Institute to pursue his calling. He also studied the concepts of Montessori education – a pedagogical approach in education that focuses on child development. Although he lacked a bachelor's degree to practice, he became a child psy-chologist – the first in Boston following the events of World War II.

The Eight Psychosocial Stages of Development

The eight stages of development below are characterized by a life-long progression. In each state, Erikson believes that we encounter crises of a psychological or a social nature. These crises are captured as es-sential questions in this chapter, and needs to be resolved before we can move to the next stage. The resolution has to be something sat-isfactory in both the psychological and the social perspectives. While this chapter discusses all stages, examples and later notes focus on the first four stages that focus on child development.

1. Mistrust vs. Basic trust (from birth to eighteen months)

During this stage, the child views the world with uncertainty. The kind of resolution a child identifies with is influenced by the kind of care that he gets from his primary relationship which focuses on the mother. Specifically, an environment of warmth, affection, positive interaction helps the child develop trust.

Application: a parent who is neglectful will likely to help a child develop mistrust to the people and the world. It should be noted that the mother and the parents are responsible in providing for a child's immediate needs. Failure to provide a regular care and affection leads to suspicion, withdrawal, frustration, and lack of confidence.

2. Shame and doubt vs. Autonomy (between eighteen months to three years)

During this stage, toddlers are busy familiarizing themselves with their bodies and what their bodies can do. This is where they learn to crawl, walk, or stand on their own – qualities that identify a sense of independence or autonomy. Hence, a supportive environment in the home needs to be present. Parents, who are the toddler's primary contact, should be supportive and loving.

Application: parents who are overprotective can hamper a child's quest towards autonomy. There are parents who refuse to let their children play on open ground, who spank their kids when they trip over or who keep their children indoor most of the time "to keep them safe." Little do parents know that a child's inquisitive nature helps him learn to not run too fast as he may trip and bruise his knees, for example.

Toilet training is also a part of this stage. A child who is always accompanied by an adult in the toilet will never learn to go on his own. This is why potties are designed for children to practice doing their thing. The only functions parents have during this stage are to render support and to help where the child encounters difficulties.

3. Initiative vs. guilt (between three to five years)

As children seek to explore the world, they are given a feeling of the need to pursue something. This need is called a purpose. Children under this stage act in order to satisfy a purpose. They learn to speak, to move from one room to another in order to get their toy, to count and to say The Alphabets, and to put on their clothes – all on their own. In contrast to giving commands, children under this stage practice to get what they want on their own because they know that they can do it.

Because actions during this stage are governed by a basic purpose, children get frustrated when they fail to achieve something. This frustration manifests in shouting, screaming, hitting, or throwing objects. The child's immediate family's role is to help channel the child's urges to socially accepted behaviors.

Application: It is common for children to mind the tasks in the kitchen. For example, if you're manually washing your dishes and your daughter wants to do it too, don't refuse her. Instead, make her wash plastic utensils so she won't break them. At the same time, explain that she should not waste water. The next time she sees an open faucet, she's turn it of and when she grows older, she'd take care of the dishes for you.

4. Industry vs. inferiority (between to five years to twelve years)

This stage is associated with school because it is during these years that we take them to nursery, kindergarten, and grade school. During these times, children to learn how to be industrious and feel the pride of accomplishing tasks at school. The school's main influencers like the teachers should encourage children to be self-reliant. At home, a child's family can help foster industry by explaining the significance of doing one's homework, stressing on the importance of education, helping the child do his homework, and praising him for a job well done.

The kind of environment at home and at school should be nurturing and encouraging. If a child is placed in an environment where his abilities and accomplishments are not recognized, are belittled, or are totally ignored, he might develop a sense of inferiority and lack of confidence in his abilities.

Application: Parents don't need to give material rewards if their children come home with stars on their hands, on their foreheads, or in their paper. Parents also don't need to buy their children a smartphone in exchange for an A. Encouragements seem to do little but it actually works inside. When children are praised, they feel proud of their accomplishments. Hence, showing the star or the A paper to everyone in the family gives the needed boost for the child to continuously perform.

5. Identity vs. identity confusion (adolescence)

As the child moves through adolescence, he will try new things, assume new roles, and acquire new behaviors. He will be with friends and will follow people he admires and respects. These actions point to the need to have a sense of identity which is motivated by having a place in the world. The success the adolescent has in forming new relationships helps cement his sense of identity. Failure to do so results in confusion and insecurity.

Application: Parents are right about monitoring the kind of people their children hang out with. One way to get to know the kind of friends teens hang out with is for parents to encourage their child to bring them home. Without being judgmental, parents can then remind their children to choose their friends wisely. A mix of friends is helpful especially when it comes to helping teens make the right choices in which group of people to follow. In return, the example set by parents to their children when it comes to who to trust and who to be cautious with affects the manner at which children perceive people's characters and influence.

6. Intimacy vs. isolation (young adulthood)

As adolescents move to adulthood, they'll soon face major phases in their life that includes forming intimate relationships. Their ability to form this kind of relationship leads them to attain intimacy with a partner. Failure to do so leads to feelings of isolation.

7. Stagnation vs. Generativity (middle adulthood)

When young adults reach mid-adulthood, they'll develop a need to create or to nurture what will be their contribution to society. This contribution usually outlasts the individual and is driven by a greater sense of purpose, and includes attaining a meaningful career. Those who aren't able to resolve the crisis involving their significance in life will end up being disconnected and would feel useless.

8. Integrity vs. despair (late adulthood until death)

The final stage in Erikson's theory involves a period of reflection. This reflection is rooted in meaning, and deals with the feelings of peace, fulfillment, and most of all, wisdom. Those who consider their life as a failure will feel despair and regret.

Tips to Parents or Caregivers

Now you know that each psychosocial stage involves a crisis that needs to be resolved, you fairly have an idea about what your "tasks" are. Remember that you don't need to memorize the different stages and everything that go with it. The only important thing is for you to realize your importance. These tips will help you.

☐ Support your children

Children will imitate you so there are times when they'll insist on doing things on their own. This kind of insistence marks that your child is working towards being independent. When faced with these situations, give your children the space they need and come in to help if they find things difficult. In addition, you should direct their sense of independence and initiative to complete tasks that produce positive effects.

☐ Talk to your children

Never encourage your children to talk only to judge them in the end. Instead, help them with their issues by going through the different options that help solve their problems. If they end up sticking to the wrong kind of people, don't hastily restrain them from hanging out with such groups. Instead, as your children begin to socialize, always remind them to be with the right people. Tell your stories; you might have found yourself in similar situations before.

☐ Recognize your children's accomplishments

There are parents who quietly celebrate their children's milestones. There are some who show them to the world. Your pride about the good thing they've done is important in giving children to feel confident about what they can do. If you criticize them, you're de-motivating them to try again. Introduce rewards that do not focus much on material things. Instead, add to the privileges they can enjoy without much spending. For example, if they get an A on their quiz, they can play video games all day on the weekend.

☐ Wait for your children

Sometimes, we know that our children are going through some problems. This is especially observable among teenagers. However, their belief that they can manage sometimes makes it difficult for us to reach out. We even end up arguing in the end. To avoid this from happening, we should encourage self-expression by establishing an atmosphere of support and letting them know that their parents are their confidantes. And then let's wait for them to open up to us. On the other hand, we can proactively tell them our stories. These are the times when we've experienced the same thing. If our teens will feel a degree of identification, they'll gradually open up.

Chapter 5:

What Kids Learn by Imitating Their Parents?

Parenting is harder these days because of the following factors:

1. Technology

New technologies, social networks, and privacy laws allow our children more private conversations and secrecy, which makes them think think that they are more wiser than they really are. We also live in an age of desk and road rage where adults can't hold themselves together—and our kids are watching.

2. Inflexible education system

We engage with an education system that has a one-size-fits-all mentality. There are standards expected for different age groups but that is no help to parents of children who have rather unique qualities and can't effectively fit in with the system. The child who thinks differently, or worse, thinks relatively slower will most likely become an outcast. It is hard, if not downright painful, being the parent of a child who is struggling mentally, academically, or socially.

3. Difficult economy

Another major factor contributing to the difficulty of parenting is the economy. School fees and the costs are increasing. This can result to some parents settling for lesser quality education, or worse--lesser quality of care.

An entire industry had been built to further add to the pressures of parents. Nowadays a plethora of businesses exist to encourage parents that their children need this and their children need that. Examples are drama schools, dance studios, music franchises, summer camps, after-school programs, outdoor education camps, extra academic tuition. Although they have tangible value to a child's development, if you are a parent who is on a tight budget, you can come to a point where you think, "isn't school supposed to be enough?"

4. Materialism

Another factor is the promotion of materialism. Our culture has popularized the acquisition of material goods with the 'He who dies with the most toys wins' T-shirt slogan. It's hard to teach children not to want, want, want when the adverts are yelling buy, buy, buy. We are programmed to want. We are not aware of it, but are constantly told to do so. Wanting is big business and more than ever parents are pressured to keep up with rapidly changing technology, trends and fashions that make life easier, more comfortable, and less scary.

With materialism comes hedonism--which is one of the worst factors that make parents' jobs a whole lot tougher! Not only are children nowadays greedy for stuff. They are also greedy for experience--wild experience. The world has promoted partying to an extremely unhealthy amount in recent years and it seems that it won't be stopping anytime soon. Rarely does the world teach self-control and restraint in this era. Without self-discipline there can be no sense of self-worth. Buddhist writer, Sakyong Mipham Rinpoche, talks about self-aggression as being the opposite of self-respect and self-worth.

5. Parental factors

You, as parents, are your children's very first and most influential role models. They literally absorb your overt and subtle behaviors, attitudes, mannerisms and expressions. Thus, what your kids experience from you and your spouse will most likely affect their identity and personality development.

Where there's constant yelling, shutting people down and fighting for the right to be heard in a family, it's not surprising when kids try what they see and hear at home in the classroom and the playground.

Modelling appropriate behavior when angry is a powerful tool that you as a parent have in influencing your kids to control angry impulses.

If the child always sees an angry face and hears an angry voice, that's the way he's likely to react when life lets him down. Remember that your kids learn by imitation and he will copy you when it comes to expressing his own anger

It's challenging when your kids' explosion stirs angry feelings within you. It's natural to get angry but this should not prevent you from responding to your child in a loving, understanding and constructive manner. How do you do it?

Communicate to your child only after your angry feelings.

A parent's immediate expression of anger toward a child can trigger a number of emotional responses in the child including guilt, fear, shame, anxiety and intense anger.

It is important not to give in quickly to the expression of anger. Instead, try to reflect inwardly. This way, you are more careful not to humiliate or shame your kids when giving a correction.

If you find that your children aren't afraid of you when you are angry, they will feel safe and are more receptive to the lessons you are trying to teach.

Identify problems that are contributing to your anger.

Are there unresolved hurts in your past that you haven't got over from? Take steps to heal yourself so you can better model emotional health. Also identify present situations that fuel your anger like dissatisfaction with job, frustration with spouse, or financial issues.

Always remember that when they are younger, your children don't usually understand that your anger isn't about them at all. The danger is that kids often take it personally. They will feel that mom or dad is always angry and doesn't love them.

Be mindful of how you talk to your child.

If you try to teach your kids to do the right thing but are overly critical of them, they are likely to develop fear and insecurity from being constantly judged. They are likely to be angry for not being able to meet unrealistic standards demanded of them.

Resist the urge to overprotect. Parents definitely mean well when they overprotect their kids but even loving parents can make children a prisoner of their own home without being aware of doing so. If you smother your kids, repeatedly question their judgment and never trust them to do things on their own, you are inviting resentment.

Children are programmed to explore as much as they possibly can. Being forced to hold back their pure unadulterated need for exploration prevents the kids from developing confidence, having fun and handling situations on their own.

Remember that one of the things that kids explode about is not being able to solve problems. Children who are been overly pampered by their parents will not gain the knowledge and experience to solve problems. So, ask yourself if your fears, worries and desire to make your child's life stress-free are stifling your kid's happiness and growth.

Shield your kids from parental conflicts

Kids learn how to communicate with others by copying how their parents get along with each other. It is very harmful for a child to be exposed to angry interactions between parents such as yelling and screaming, put downs, blaming, harsh criticisms, sarcastic remarks, and threats of harm and intimidation.

Parents should learn to restrain themselves and to control their emotions when kids are present. It's essential to avoid putting your children in the middle of your fights.

Make anger your ally

Your kid's anger can give you a helpful insight about yourself and your parenting style. Sometimes, understanding your child's anger can help you better understand and heal your own angry past.

Is your child reacting in the same way you did as a child? Maybe you're doing the same things your own parents were doing that infuriated you when you were a kid. This is a good time to reflect.

Challenges build character

Our children are raised in a media soup of messages that show teens abusing parents and modeling bad behavior. Television programs like World's Strictest Parents, Super Nanny and many of the reality, crime and police programs portray kids acting badly. These shows are hallmarks of a culture that is fascinated by rock-bottom standards, and they demonstrate how hard it is for people in positions of authority to set and maintain boundaries. This is not empowering for parents as our kids watch with eyes wide open. You might ban watching these programs on television in your home but your kids can, and will, trawl the internet to feed their curiosity if that is what interests them. Media thrives on sensationalism; entertainment that was once considered fun by today's adult generation--which is about family, perseverance, hard work--is no longer endearing to children..

You simply cannot switch off all the media and marketing that influences your child. Parenting is definitely more challenging these days—and the problem is you just can't stop; you have to carry on.

Chapter 6:

Managing Kids' Anger about Divorce

Nobody usually really wants a divorce, but if it is inevitable, it pays to keep in mind how it affects your kids.

When parents get divorced, their children justifiably feel hurt at being let down by parents who are supposed to protect them from pain. They typically mask the pain with anger and aggressive behavior. Kids are normally conflicted in their emotions toward each of their parents. Some of these emotions include anger at one parent for leaving, fear that the other parent will leave too, and guilt over the belief that they somehow caused their parents separation.

Often, kids don't express their anger openly at their parents. Instead, they act out in school, fight with their siblings or lock themselves in their bedrooms.

The good news is that children are highly adaptive and resilient in nature and can cope with separation and divorce if you create opportunities to relieve the pain from their young hearts.

Divorce is understandably difficult for you and you may find it hard to have the energy to deal with your kids' anger issues. Start by taking care of yourself so you can be there for your kids. If you need to vent out your anger and frustration to a support group or a therapist so you don't take it out on your kids, do so.

The best thing you can do for your kids if you're undergoing a divorce is offer your presence, unconditional love and reassurance. Understand that your kids' anger and anxiety are normal reactions to this big change happening in their lives.

Listen to your kids

You may not be able to change your kids feeling of sadness and frustration to happiness but acknowledging what they feel and encouraging them to express their sadness and frustration help them make peace with the situation. Kids need to know someone cares enough to hear them out.

Don't dismiss whatever your kids have to say. Build trust by assuring them that they don't have to hold back in talking about their honest feelings. If you see that they have difficulty expressing themselves, help them find words for their feelings.

Clear up misunderstandings

For divocees, always remind your kids as often as you need to that they are not responsible for the divorce. Explain to them why you decided to get a divorce without overwhelming them with the details. Hearing the real reason can help kids to understand. However, you need to choose carefully how much information to tell them. Older kids may need more details while younger kids do better with a simple explanation. Never provide details of the other parent's behavior or make your kids feel that they have to choose between you and the other parent.

Also set proper expectations to your kids about changes in their living arrangements, school and activities. The most important thing that your kid need to know that no matter how different things are going to be, you and your spouse will love him the way you've always did.

Watch out for signs of more serious problems

Expect that it will take some time for your kids to come to terms with the divorce or separation. However, if you don't see gradual improve-ment over several months, or behaviors become extreme, do your kids a favor and get professional help. Child therapists help hundreds or thousands of families go through this process and a good profes-sional can be valuable in helping your kids cope and move on.

Here are some red flags that tell you your kids might need profes-sional help:

☐ Long periods of sadness

☐ Trouble at school

☐ Withdrawn behavior

☐ Changes in daily habits

☐ Frequent violent outbursts or temper tantrums

☐ Poor concentration

☐ Self-injury and eating disorders

☐ Taking anger out to other children

☐ Feeling anxious or worried

If these problems start suddenly after the divorce and you feel that their actions are a bit too extreme, getting extra help is im

Chapter 7:

How Favoritism Provokes Kids to Anger

Playing favorites encourages high levels of anger and aggression within sibling relationships. When parents favor one child over another, the less-favored child carries around feelings of not being good enough which damages his self-worth. It also negatively affects the favored child who will soon feel the resentment of his siblings and can ultimately make him hate being the star child.

Your kids tend to sense easily when you're playing favorites. You must guard against anything that would result in your children developing feelings of being "less worthy" than their siblings.

Try these ways to keep harmony and fairness in your home:

☐ Do not compare siblings

A child being constantly told "Why can't you be like your brother/sister?" can develop lasting resentment, jealousy and low self-esteem. Statements of comparison can discourage a sibling from even trying because he feels like he could never keep up with his favored sibling.

Praising one kid's behavior in contrast to a sibling puts unfair pressure on the one you praised and belittles the other.

☐ Do not take sides in a fight

One of the reasons why one sibling feels his mom or dad favors his brother or sister is when parents get involved in their quarrels. Unfortunately, parents tend to see one child as being in the wrong and punish that child while sparing the other.

If you want to avoid showing favoritism, listen openly to all sides. After all, it takes two cooperating to make a fight. If you have to punish, punish both siblings equally. For example, if two siblings can't share the PlayStation without fighting, both don't get to play with it. If they bicker over who gets to wear the pink dress, neither of them could.

☐ Listen to unfairness complaints when they arise

You don't have to drive yourself crazy trying to make it "fair" all the time. Sometimes your kids' "it's not fair" complaints arise from trying to manipulate you to give in to their wants. But sometimes, the complaining child is really asking for attention and approval from you that he is truly missing.

Spend alone time with each child

Spending special alone time with each of your kids is an excellent way to make them feel treasured. It also gives you better insight into your child's unique traits and personality. It helps you figure out how you can be more responsive to your child.

The best antidote for favoritism is to favor all your children. It's critical that all children feel loved and highly prized for what makes them unique and special. Make them understand that they are all appreciated for their individuality and because of this, they should not feel the need to be better from their siblings because all of them are special.

Chapter 8:

Anger Triggered by the Pain of Rejection

Rejection hurts. It's one of the most distressing experiences in life. We are hardwired to react with anger and sadness when we are rejected or threatened with rejection. It's especially devastating for kids who thrive on feelings of recognition and acceptance. Feeling that he is not liked is enough to make a   child's world collapse.

Children experience rejection in so many ways - being picked last for a basketball team, being called names, not being invited to a party, or being ignored deliberately by peers. Children who can't cope with rejection can misdirect resentment toward his siblings or his parents.

If your child's anger is triggered by being excluded and having a difficult time getting along with peers, help your child to move beyond this negative experience by being there to talk and listen to him, validate his feelings and navigate the struggles in his relationships. Here are the "supportive actions" that you can do:

1. Help your child find his own ways of coping

Do not jump in to save your child from every upsetting experience. Being over involved and overprotective only makes your child dependent on you and unable to bounce back from any rejection he may experience.

Support your child's independence by showing faith that he will recover from the sting of rejection. Every time your child overcomes challenges and setbacks, he actually grows stronger.

Be patient. It takes time to develop social skills and resilience to rise above rejections and challenges. Remember that your child's anger is just a symptom of a deeper disappointment. You focus is not to restrain anger but to build your child's confidence to help him get through rough times without exploding and hurting other people.

Help your child to realize that if he does not resolve his anger from a particular hurt, this anger can damage friendships and can limit participation in sports and other group activities.

2. Examine your child's behaviors that may push away friends

Everyone gets left out by friends from time to time and usually, they get over it. But if criticism and rejection happen to your child once too often, your child may be acting in ways that are off-putting to his peers. Here are some common behaviors that make it hard for your kids to be accepted by peers:

☐ Bragging

☐ Being oblivious to others reaction

☐ Being a poor sport

☐ Trying so hard to be funny

☐ Ways to help your child improve social relationships:

Instead of bragging to impress friends, discover with your child what he shares in common with peers and help him create ways to make friends with classmates with shared interests.

Help your child pick up on social cues to stop a behaviour that annoys his peers. You may need to tell your child that a friend looking away or walking away can mean that he has lost interest in a topic and can be a sign to stop talking.

Help your child build tolerance for losing in games by encouraging him to have fun playing games with friends win or lose.

If you believe that your child is better off trying to be kind than funny, come up with possible opportunities for acts of kindness to try at school.

3. Help your kids accept unchangeable features in their lives

One of the challenges young children face is when they are ridiculed because of physical appearance, race, mental capabilities and family background. Being mocked as a person is a devastating blow to a child's self-esteem. This can cause the child to disown himself and feel shame for who he is.

Unless kids come to terms with it, these unchangeable features will remain as tension points that will continue to trigger bouts of anger while growing up.

It is important to reinforce the positive aspects of your child's appearance. Help your child embrace who he is. Get rid of the shame and clean out the "I am ugly", "I am bad", "I'm not worthy" belief implanted on your child's consciousness.

Chapter 9:

Understanding Your Child's Temperament

Misfits and rebels

A common parenting problem is the child who is ruthless—who esca-lates and takes things a step too far. If you take a toy off him, he will hit you. If you confiscate the computer, she will take something precious of yours and destroy it.

When our kids don't comply with what is considered 'normal' in our educational, medical or social system it creates an enormous problem for the parents. I doubt you would be reading this book if you weren't in some way concerned about your child and how he or she fits in.

If you do happen to be in those lonely shoes right now I want to etch this thought firmly in your mind: You can handle this, you are meant to handle this and you will prevail. I am not promising you 'easy' but there is a way forward and the key to that is within you. It may also help to know that you are not alone. Let me introduce you to some others who have struggled also.

I mentored one woman whose child would undoubtedly have been diagnosed with a borderline personality disorder if she had taken him to a doctor but she didn't want him to be labeled and didn't believe the doctors could help. Her 15-year-old son would not participate in conversation and had no social life except his online gaming pals. He disliked talking to other people and if badgered by his parents he would act out like bumping his mother as he passed her in the hallway or in the kitchen. She was afraid to confront him in case the violence escalated.

Another couple had a 17-year-old who had dropped out of school and refused to get out of bed and do anything. It is easy to say 'the parents should make him' but when the boy is bigger than they are that's eas-ier said than done. 'Well, don't feed him then' some might say. These parents didn't feed him but when they went to work he got out of bed and raided the fridge. 'They should kick him out' others might say. But when his friends are druggies and dropouts is that really what you would do? 'They should send him off to do military service.' Er, how? Are they meant to drag an 80 kg youth out of the car into the induction area? What's the Sergeant Major going to say to that?

It is easy to blame the parents when parents are just one influence on their children. But blame the parents is what we do. It makes us feel superior and then we can believe that 'they brought it on themselves', so we do not need to get involved. We think we can wash our hands of the problem and forget that we are all part of the whole. The world is a 'melting pot' and social behavior is viral. Humans are social animals and we learn by mimicking others. Someone starts planking; thousands start doing it. One kid takes Dad's car without permission; others think they can do the same. Miley Cyrus starts twerking and toddlers seeing the clip follow suit.

If you are troubled by your kids' behavior the first step away from struggle is to understand how small the part you play in this is. You may be feeling sad, worried, and guilty, feeling like it is all your fault or that you have failed when the big picture is this:

☐ Your child is not you

☐ Your child was born with their own spirit and life dreams

☐ Our children are exposed to media and marketing, and influence from their peers, schools, religions, government health programs, and charitable foundations with 'educational' messages and all the power of the international entertainment industry.

The problem is, sometimes help is harder to find because the older child or teenager is no longer a cute youngster and the problems are somewhat louder, bigger and messier. To realize you need help and then have the courage to ask for it is a sign of strength, not weakness.

Your job as a parent is to do your best—no one can do more than that—and call out for help when you need it. New parents are urged to get help when they have a newborn but that advice holds true when your child is older, perhaps even more so.

We are all connected, and to not see that is naïve. We see that in our classrooms when the whole class suffers because one child can't control his behavior. We are reminded of that as we comb nits out of our child's hair or when we find out our child has followed the leader in a drinking binge.

When you have a child you join the melting pot, and even if you try to isolate yourself from it, resistance is futile, your efforts to resist will still create its own unique experiences. And all of this is, perhaps, a good thing because having a child extends you and develops your spirit. Having a child makes you real.

While a child's angry behavior is usually triggered by frustrating events in his life, it may also be influenced by his own temperament. Your child is born with a preferred style of reacting to the world around him.

An important question you should be asking is "who is my child, and how can I be more responsive to the hand I've been dealt?" When you understand your child's temperament, you can work with him more easily in finding ways to improve his chance of successfully dealing with his emotions and life's challenges.

Many scientific studies have continued to show that temperament greatly influences kids' development. Observe how your kids react to each situation to gain insights of their behavioural tendencies.

The 9 temperament traits

These 9 temperament traits are developed based on a research conducted by Doctors Alexander Thomas and Stella Chess:

Activity Level: the extent of your child's motor activity. Is your child generally moving and doing something or is content to sit quietly and prefer activities not requiring much physical activities? Highly active kids need help in channelling their energy. This may be through dancing or sporty activities.

Adaptability: how your child adapts to changes in his environment. Does your child quickly adapt to new situations or does it take a long time to be comfortable with changes in routines? Slow-to-adapt kids need to know what's going to happen and usually need time to shift from one activity to another. They are not being stubborn, they're just cautious. And they need your support. On the other hand, kids who jump into things quickly need to be taught to think and then act before they find themselves in dangerous situations.

Persistence: your child's attention span and persistence in an activity. Does your child move on to another activity in the face of a tough challenge or does he continue to work on the activity until he gets it right? Persistent kids may be negatively labelled as stubborn because they usually persist in an activity even though they're asked to stop. Kids with low persistence may find it easier to develop strong social skills because they recognize that they can get help from other people.

Intensity: the energy level of responses whether positive or negative. Does your child react strongly to everything or tend to get quiet when upset? Intense kids need help in learning how to calm themselves. They may be quite exhausting to deal with because of the depth of their emotion. If you identify that your child's reaction can be intense, you may want to expose him in the dramatic arts.

Mood: your child's tendency to react to situations in a positive or negative way. Is your child generally happy or serious? Is he generally even-tempered or does his mood shift easily? Serious kids tend to carefully evaluate situations.

Regularity: the predictability of your child's biological functions like eating and sleeping. Does your child gets hungry or tired at predictable times or is somewhat irregular in his eating and sleeping habits? Regular kids need predictable routines while irregular kids need flexibility.

Distractibility: the degree of your child's concentration. How easily is your child distracted? Does he become sidetracked easily when working on some activity? It may be easier to divert an easily-distracted child from an undesirable behaviour. On the other hand, it may be difficult for him to finish an important assignment.

Sensory threshold: your child's sensitivity to physical stimuli. Does your child react positively or negatively to sounds, temperature, taste and touch? Sensitive kids are easily bothered by sensations.

Approach/Withdrawal: your child's response to a new object or person. Does your child accept a new experience or withdraws from it? Slow-to-warm up kids are resistant when faced with new things, people or situations. They are less likely to act impulsively.

The 9 temperament traits

There are 3 basic types of temperaments formed by a combination of the 9 temperament traits: easy, difficult, and cautious.

The easy child is generally calm and in a positive mood. He quickly establishes regular routines and adapts easily to new environment.

The easy child rarely demands attention. Because of this, it may be necessary for you to intentionally set aside special time to talk to your child about his pain, frustrations and struggles because he won't ask for it.

The difficult child tends to react negatively, engages in irregular habits, gets easily troubled by sensations, displays intense emotions and is fearful of new people and experiences.

You may need to make a number of accommodations for your difficult child including providing opportunities that allow him to work off stored up energy, being flexible with setting up routines and indentifying the sensations that bother him.

The cautious or slow-to-warm up child has a low activity level, tends to withdraw, reacts negatively to new situations and displays low intensity of mood. But if he is constantly exposed to constructive situations, his reactions eventually become more positive.

Be patient with this kind of child. Allow him ample time to accept new situations and establish new relationships.

Adapting to your child's temperament

If you have determined your child's unique temperament, you also need to be aware of your own temperament traits and identify areas that conflict with your child. This way, you can make the first move to adapt and adjust your parenting methods in order to avoid clash of temperaments between you and your child.

When you understand your own temperament and your child's, you're not left in the dark. You can better understand the needs and emotions each of you is experiencing.

One very important thing to keep in mind is to accept and focus on the hand your holding not on what you wish your child should be. You may long for an easy child but you gave birth to a moody and inflexible child. You have to accept this reality and be a positive guide to your child's natural way of responding to his environment.

Chapter 10:

Why Anger Management Helps Temperamental Kids

Anger management for a child may seem strange or perhaps even downright ridiculous to others, but when you are the parent of a temperamental child it can be a lifesaver. In this chapter, we are going to talk a little bit about the benefits of anger management and what it can do to help to bring your child manage his anger better

1. Developing Positive Social Skills

With a proper anger management counselor as well as proper anger management work at home, children who commonly have anger management problems can easily develop positive social skills. Anger management helps children to develop these more positive skills by implementing a number of exercises that help the temperamental child to become more self-aware.

2. Improved Learning in School

Anger management is designed to not only work with children through their emotions, but it is also designed to teach children about socially acceptable ways of acting. With knowledge of how to behave in social situations – even when angry – your child will not only thrive more at school, but they will also experience less resistance from their peers. Research shows that children who are angry and who act out are often the same children who get left out by peers or even picked on.

3. Developing a Proper Understanding of Emotions

Anger management not only teaches children how to better handle their anger and their emotions, but it also helps children to better understand their emotions. With a better grasp on feelings and emotions, children will be able to better grasp the concept of acceptable and unacceptable behavior as well.

4. Confront your denial

Society broadcasts the ideal of the 'happy family' and at some level most of us subscribe to that belief, so when our lives don't reflect that paradigm there is disappointment, a sense of failure and for some a sense of shame.

If you and your child are disconnected and you are feeling heartache it is time to own the situation you are in right now. Denial won't help. Avoiding thinking about it, hoping it will go away on its own, or finding something else to do instead are coping strategies but they are not healing strategies.

Often we go into denial because we feel overwhelmed. By not admitting that our problem needs fixing we can pretend that we are okay. However, always remember that your children should come first. That means you should not be defeated by your emotions. You should focus on the fact that you have to confront your child's anger because it will help him develop.

5. Teaching Children How to Make Better Choices

Anger management is a great way to teach children how to make better choices in their life. It teaches them how to stop and think about their emotions before acting, and it also teaches them to take a time out when needed. Anger management is an optimal tool and when implemented by both a parent and an anger management professional it can set your child up for success in managing their emotions as well as how they act out.

Chapter 11:

Anger Management Methods for Temperamental Kids

In the chapter above, we discussed the benefits of anger management for temperamental children, in this chapter we are going to cover some anger management approaches that you can take at home. While it is definitely always a good idea to bring in a professional counselor to tackle anger in children, that is not to say that there are not methods that you can implement at home to supplement the work that your child's counselor is doing in therapy

1. Teach Your Child Problem Solving Skills

Problem-solving skills are an imperative part of being able to work through anger or even avoid it. You can help your child to do this by teaching them a variety of skills that they can implement when they feel themselves starting to get angry. A great way to do this is to sit down with your child and ask for their opinion on how they would solve each problem that occurs that would usually make them feel angry. You can also offer your own opinion on how you would solve problems that lead to you or your child getting angry as well.

2. Teach Your Child What is an Acceptable Behavior

At some point in our life, we all learn what acceptable behavior is, we learn this from our environment as well as from our parents. Being able to identify what is acceptable and what is not acceptable behavior is what helps us to learn how to act even when our feelings are telling us to act otherwise. The best way to teach your child about acceptable behavior is to spend some time talking about feelings and talking about how your child would like you to act in public when you feel the same way that they have when they feel angry.

3. Teach Your Child How to Relax

Being able to relax is what helps most of us to let go of our angry feelings or even prevent them from building up in the first place. It is your responsibility as a parent to teach your child how to relax. Some good methods to teach your child how to relax include yoga, sitting down with their favorite toy, taking deep breaths, walking away from anger cues and talking about their feelings.

4. Teach Your Child to Recognize Cues to Their Anger

We all have things that make us angry; these things are called "cues", and as we get older we become more adept at recognizing these cues. It is your job as your child's parent to teach your child to recognize the cues that make them angry so that they can avoid them in the future. Being able to avoid cues will help your child to reduce their anger and minimize their outbursts.

5. Help Your Child to Build a Positive Self Image

Anger can be a difficult emotion for children and often times it can lead to a negative self-image. As your child's parent, it is your responsibility to teach your child that anger is a natural emotion and that it does not mean that they are a bad person. One way to do this is to sit down with your child and talk about their anger, discuss how everyone gets angry at times and how it is a perfectly natural feeling. Also make some time to discuss how with your child how he should be expressing his emotions. This actually helps a great deal.

Chapter 12:

Methods for You to Cope With an Angry Child

We have just covered some of the approaches that you can take to help your child to cope with their anger and assimilate back into acceptable behavior. This time, we are going to focus on you. Below you will find some methods that you can keep in mind to help you to deal with your angry child to help to preserve your own sanity

1. Don't Yell at Your Child When They Are Angry

It can be easy to yell at your child when they are angry, after all, their anger makes us angry. The problem is, however, that once you begin yelling at an angry child, they are going to yell back, and things are quickly going to turn into a shouting match. It is much more effective instead to sit and talk quietly with your child or to wait out their anger before talking to them in a normal tone of voice about their behavior.

2. Don't Try to Reason with an Angry Child

When your child becomes angry, it is important to take a moment to let your child calm down before trying to reason with them. Trying to reason with an angry child is not only an exercise in futility, but it is also an exercise that can be just as frustrating for you as it is for your child. Instead of reasoning with a child when they are angry, take a time out for yourself while your child works through their feelings and once they begin to calm down, sit down quietly and with closeness between you, reason with your child about their behavior.

3. Don't Get Physical

As adults living in a society that is overrun with violence, we can sometimes be tempted to spank our children or otherwise physically discipline them when they are acting poorly. You absolutely should never do this! Getting physical with your child is never a good idea for numerous reasons, instead, remind yourself that you are much older than your child and much bigger and it is important that you don't act out of anger towards them for fear of truly hurting them. You are much stronger than your child is and as the adult you should be able to reason your way out of a situation rather than bring physical harm to your child.

4. Don't Freeze

Some of us are not built for conflict and in these circumstances we are often led to freezing up when our children act poorly. It is important with children not to freeze up like this because you not only give your child more time to act poorly, but you also let your child know that you are not in control of the situation. One way to help yourself when you feel as though you are going to freeze up is to stop and take a couple of deep breaths. Remind yourself of how important it is to be a healthy role model for your child as well as how important it is that you teach your child how to react when someone acts poorly to them.

5. Only Give Consequences for Bad Behavior

Giving consequences for bad behavior versus giving consequences for anger itself is an important part of teaching children how to manage their behavior and how to understand their emotions. By punishing bad behavior, you are teaching your child that it is okay to feel anger but it is not okay to behave badly because of that anger. If, however, you punish your child for their bad behavior and for being angry, your child will become emotionally constipated and be reluctant to feel anger at even appropriate times in the future. It is also possible that by punishing anger, your child will associate anger with being punished and spend their life feeling guilty whenever they get angry.

6. Don't Overly Punish Your Child

When our child acts out and makes us angry, we can sometimes go overboard with our punishment. Overly punishing a child because of their anger-related behavior is unfair and rather than teaching our children how to de-escalate their behavior, it often teaches our children to become angrier and that it is okay to lash out. If you feel that you are in danger of overly punishing your child, try asking someone else to help you to make an appropriate punishment or take time out before assigning your child's punishment.

7. Take a Time Out

Sometimes it is important not for your child to take a time out, but for you to take a time out. It is easy enough to get worked up along with our children, to want to shout and scream and act like a child, but it is important that you maintain your cool head so when needed take a time out. Whether you leave your child with a friend or family member or whether you simply redirect your attention to something else, redirecting yourself with a timeout can help you to calm down and refocus.

8. Keep In Mind That You Are a Role Model

It can be very difficult to keep in mind that you are your child's role model when you are facing a temper tantrum of epic proportions, but it is crucial that you do so. Your child depends on you to give them a role model, to explain and exhibit how best to express their emotions, and you are not doing this if you are allowing yourself to act out. So the next time that you feel like acting out in unison with your child, remember that they are going to mimic what they learn from you, so it is your job to act like an adult and manage your own emotions properly.

9. Use Closeness

Closeness is an important factor in helping you deal with your temperamental child. While the last thing you probably feel like doing when your child is angry and acting out, it is one of the best ways that you can help to comfort your child when they are experiencing extreme emotions. Closeness can be as simple as sitting down next to your child and talking to them softly about their emotions, or it can involve holding or even restraining your child. Restraint, although somewhat extreme, can be the only way to help a child to calm down when they are physically violent toward themselves or others.

10. Teach Your Child about Verbally Expressing Feelings

One difficulty that many temperamental children have is the inability to express their feelings verbally. As your child's parent, it is important to teach your child how to do this through various exercises. One way that you can begin to work with your child to identify emotions is through utilizing flashcards designed to help children with visual cues to emotion. These cards help children to tell you how they feel based on images of the human face. Another way to help children to verbally express their feelings is to have them to verbally identify their emotions as they are feeling them. You can help to do this by identifying your own emotions verbally and then requesting that your child do the same.

Chapter 13:

Positive Reinforcement Method

The words "positivity" and "creativity" are important words if they are used correctly. When you work on raising your child to become creative and positive, you not only help your child, but you help the society as well.

Role Model

The first source that has a big effect on your child is you; the parent. When your child sees you as being creative and handle different situations in a positive way, then without a doubt, he will learn these skills from you.

Therefore, let me mention to you some of the attributes that you need to cultivate in yourself so your child can learn from you and make them part of his personality.

1. Smile

As you know, smiling is contagious. When you smile, you not only improve your current mood, but you also affect the other folks that you deal with. You need to have a smile on most of the time, especially when you deal with your child. When your child sees a smile on your face, he will begin to build this good habit in himself from an early age.

2. Avoid vulgar and negative remarks

You need to avoid vulgar and negative remarks and instead use polite, uplifting statements as complaining will teach your child to complain at the slightest matters.

3. Optimism

You need to start handling situations in an optimistic way, especially when your child is present with you. Encourage your child to tackle different situations in a positive way and keep reminding him that he is destined to succeed in life; if he puts his mind to it.

What often happens is that parents ingrain pessimism in children with-out realizing it. If your child sees you complain that there is no enough money for example, he will start to develop a lack mentality.

Instead, you need to help your child believe that there is abundance and start focusing on the solutions whenever you encounter a chal-lenge, so your child can learn these positive thinking habits from you.

4. Good Behavior

Treat others respectfully and deal with them fairly, especially in front of your child. The child, in his first years watches his parents how they deal with salesmen, neighbors, and friends. Remember, by watching you, he is able to learn how to behave with others.

Therefore, you need to build good manners in your child since an early age and you can accomplish that by being a good role model.

5. Become spiritual

You might be surprised that I mention spirituality in here, but it is the most important trait you can teach your child. When you behave in front of your child in a spiritual, practical way, he will begin to trust their intuition and inner power. Your child will learn how to make the law of multiple returns work for him.

The law of multiple returns states that when you give out anything such as money, you will achieve multiples in return if you really be-lieve what you say and trust God in the process.

Many children nowadays grow with having a lack mentality whether it is the belief in lack of money, lack of money, or lack of abundance. In order to develop an abundant mentality, you need to become more spiritual and begin to appreciate what you have, so your child can learn to do the same.

Chapter 14:

Optimism

Optimism is an important attribute to have and it will help you raise your child as a positive and well-mannered individual. That's why there's a whole chapter in this book that is designated for it. When your child hears optimistic and uplifting conversations, then hope and optimism will become part of his thought pattern. Therefore, it is crucial that you encourage such kind of environment for your child.

This can be difficult nowadays because of all the negative issues that you can find. However, you need to teach your child that there is still good in the world and that he can thrive in any circumstances that he encounters. You also need to help your child interpret situations in a positive way. Inform your child that there is at least two ways to look at situations, one positive and one negative. Therefore, it is more beneficial to choose the positive interpretation because it will serve you better.

Your child needs to see examples, not just hear you giving lectures to him. Therefore, you need to begin to interpret situations and problems in a skillful and positive way in front of them, so they can learn from your experience.

So how do you raise your child to be an optimist?

1. Find out how your child tends to think

When something happens to his disliking, does he usually get upset quickly, or he tends to be calm? Does he let small issues affect his day and ruin his good mood? If you notice that he tends to be pessimistic, help him to become optimistic and see the bright side of things.

2. Face pessimism with your child

If your child tends to expect bad things to happen to him, then help him to work on this thought pattern. For example, if he usually says, "No one in the class likes me," help him change that negative thought to positive "There are many kids that will like you. You are fun, polite, and have sense of humor." Programming your child on a daily basis that he is unique and wonderfully made is an important part in the process.

3. Give your child an optimism class

Your child will experience some negative situations as everyone will. The trick is to help him view these negative situations as temporary and that they are necessary part of growth. Help your child to not take these setbacks personal.

4. Help your child face his negative self-talk

Negative self-talk is detrimental, especially to a child. Therefore, you need to help your child develop positive self-talk. One of the best ways to do this is by using a three step process that many therapists use to reduce pessimism in people. These three step process are called NED which stand for Notice, Externalize, and Dispute. Notice negative self-talk. Externalize it! Treat self-talk as if it were said by someone else who is main goal to see you fail. Dispute it in the same way you would do to any person that you don't like.

5. Show your child optimism

Do you tend to say statements like "I know that I'm going to win" or "I knew that I am not going to win! I never win at anything?" The way you handle life issues has a direct impact on your child's thinking pattern. Therefore, if you want to help your child become an optimistic, show direct examples to your child on a daily basis.

Chapter 15:

Planning

Planning is an indispensable trait that you must ingrain in your child from an early age in order for him to become productive and successful.

When you hear the word "planning," you might have connected the word with corporations, companies, and complex strategic planning. But, that is not what I mean by planning. Planning should be simple, easy, and fun. Therefore, let me give you some simple steps to help you teach your child how to plan for his life:

1. Recognize your child's hobbies and capabilities

First, you need to recognize your child's hobbies and capabilities. This can be done by analyzing his personality and by knowing what he likes and doesn't like.

☐ Does he like to play with others or alone?

☐ Is he an active child or he likes to be quiet most of the time?

☐ Does he like to watch television or not?

☐ Does he like art?

☐ Does he like to sing and play instruments?

☐ Does he like to dance?

☐ Does he like to swim?

☐ Does he like to play with cars and other objects?

All of the answers to these questions will give you a hint on what your child likes and what his interests are. You then can help him plan to develop his hobbies.

DON'T LOSE YOUR TEMPER

2. Building toys for planning

The building toys for kids are good toys to help your child develop planning skills.

Sit with your child and start building houses and cubes in various ways and explain to your child the difference between the two methods. Then he can use the same method to plan for his future and life.

Just let me remind you that you need to make the game fun so your child becomes interested in what you are trying to teach him.

3. What do you like to be?

Ask your child, "What do you want to be when you grow up?" Your child might remember a specific person or personality that he saw on the cartoons or in some of the family members. Or he might want to be like one of you; his parents.

Talk to him in a simple way and if he chooses a positive personality, help him to ingrain the traits in himself until he reaches his goal.

If your child chooses a negative personality that is against good manners, you would need to ask him why he chose that personality. Be sure not to force your child to be like you as his interests and capabilities could be different.

4. Create a grid

Teach your child to create a simple grid in which he can write what he wants to do during the day like eating times, sleeping times, playing times, studying times, etc...

Creating a grid will help him learn to plan for his day in a constructive way. Later on when he grows a little, you can teach him how to manage his time effectively.

5. Daily time

Ask your child what he would like to accomplish for the day, the week, and the month? At the beginning, the answer might be simple. Teach him to write what he wants to do as this trait will help him become organized and disciplined.

Be considerate and do not force things on to your child and watch every move he makes. On the contrary, your job is to make him like planning and make it seem as a fun activity. You can give your child a prize even if the tasks he chose are simple.

These are five tips that you can do to help your child learn this important value called "planning." The main goal as I mentioned is to develop your child to plan to his life so he can become productive and successful. If your child doesn't learn this important value, he might not be able to succeed and reach excellence; hence his productivity will be lower.

☐ Tip: The generation that knows the art of planning is positive and ambitious because the individual who plans will always be ambitious to make positive accomplishments in the society.

Chapter 16:

Independence

Independence is a concept you have to make sure that you take the time to teach your child. Today in our society, there are many children who are too dependent on the parents. Therefore, it is imperative that you teach this concept to your child from an early age.

Here are some tips to help you ingrain this value called "independence" in your child:

1. Chores

Teach your child to do chores alone such as to organize his room, clean his room, study alone, and make his own sandwiches. Of course, you would need to help him some times, especially if he is busy or need some guidance, so leave some room for flexibility.

2. Buying simple items

Train your child to buy some food from the nearby shops and restaurants. For example, you can have your child buy juice or milk from the shop or you can make him buy a sandwich from the nearby restaurant. Of course, first you would need to train him several times until he feels confident and comfortable doing the errand by himself.

3. Choose his clothes

Give him the option to decide the clothes to wear and the styles he likes. If he chooses something inappropriate, then you can take the time to chat with him about the reasons he chose this style. You would then guide him to choose appropriate clothes depending on the occasion.

4. Joining a club

Register your child in a club that is specific for children so he can learn how to exercise and take care of his health. By joining a club, he will be meet others and become independent by learning how to take care of his health.

5. Planning

Simple planning is what I described above will help your child to depend on himself, not others.

6. Traveling

Teach your child to help you when you go on vacation. You can give him the task of organizing the bedrooms as an example. This will teach him how to depend on himself and accomplish certain tasks.

7. Collaboration

You need not to forget to teach him the importance of collaboration. You wouldn't want your child to be independent and start feeling superior to others. You need to teach him that collaboration is needed at times.

Manners

One of the main factors that affect your child's productivity and success is having high manners. Abiding by high manners is a crucial aspect that you must teach your child in order for him to become positive.

The positive individual needs to be able to deal with different kinds of personalities; hence he needs to have high manners in order to win and affect their hearts.

If you are able to ingrain high manners in your child's personality, you will have succeeded in raising your child as a positive human being.

Now, let me provide you with some tips that will help you to ingrain good manners and habits in your child:

1. Honesty

This is one of the most important manners that must be ingrained in your child since honest folks tend to be more trusted than others. Remember, as the proverb says, "Honesty is the best policy."

2. Respect

Respect is another important manner since nowadays you live in a society that has many different nationalities and social status. Therefore, your child must learn to respect all nationalities, all religions, and the different races.

Respecting others helps to eliminate hatred and prejudice. It also helps your child to appreciate the differences between humans and cultures.

3. Trust worthy

You also need to teach your child to become trust worthy. For instance, you can tell a secret to your child and inform him not to tell anyone about it. If someone else asks him about the secret, he must not divulge the secret and stay quiet.

This is a great manner that is very necessary in life especially in dealing with other humans. Inform your child that if he divulges a secret, others will think less highly of him and they wouldn't trust him anymore.

4. Collaboration

Collaboration is another important trait that your child needs to learn about. Helping others when needed must be done regularly including helping his siblings and friends at school. He has to mingle and become an active participant in school and life.

You can also help your child volunteer in one of the charities to make a positive difference in someone's life or in the society. This all requires your child to collaborate with others and create something worthwhile together.

5. Giving

The art of giving is another trait that your child needs to learn about and practice doing. When you give him an allowance, teach him to save a small percentage of it and give it to charity. This characteristic will teach your child to share the good that he has with others.

6. Point out good manners in others

Start showing and pointing out examples of good manners and habits that people tend to do. For instance, if someone said to you "thank you" after helping him out, explain to your child that his individual is showing respect because you have helped him out.

By pointing out good manners to your child, your child will begin to raise his awareness to what good manners are and then he will begin developing those manners and making them a habit of his personality.

7. Practice good manners at home

Learn to practice good manners on a daily basis. When you sit on the table to eat dinner, make sure you show your child some etiquettes such as to never talk when his mouth is full and he should always clean his mouth with a napkin. Also, practice saying "Thank you" to your child whenever he gets you a glass of water or something that you have asked for. As I said earlier, you are the first source that will affect your child. By practicing good manners, you are affecting your child's behavior as he will learn from you.

Chapter 17:

Communication

Social skills are important characteristics to have. The positive indi-vidual has to mingle with others regularly, therefore, he has to have good listening skills and learn to speak eloquently.

Every parent wants to help his children develop and progress whether it is making polite friends, enjoying school, building good manners, and improving communication skills. However, sometimes, the child might not be like what the parents hope for him to be. He might be an introvert instead of an extrovert. Or he might not be able to connect with others socially.

The good news is that these skills can be worked on and enhanced. Not only will social skills help him communicate better with others, but they also will help him do better in school, build his self-confidence, and manners.

It is your responsibility to ingrain these traits in your child in order to develop a successful and productive child. To help you in this pro-cess, follow the below tips:

1. Teach your child the importance of conversations and discussion in life. Since the person meets many people on a daily basis such as in the house, school, and stores, he needs to develop these essential skills to be able to carry conversations.

2. Teaching your child to listen and not interrupt the other person while talking is crucial. This is a sign of respect and makes the other person feel important.

3. Avoiding arguments and debates is crucial. The communication must be quiet without throwing negative remarks at each other and respecting each other's view.

4. Staying on topic is crucial. Usually, children have a hard time stay-ing on topic and quick at changing subjects. To help your child focus and stay on topic, follow the below tips:

☐ Fruit games- play the fruit game in which every alphabet has to be the beginning of a fruit name such as O orange, P pears, B banana etc...

☐ Help your child to improvise- To play this game, put photos of different emotions face down on the couch. Then you and your child decide on some story elements that must appear in the story (e.g., a deer, a lion, and a forest). The goal is for the players to take turns making up the narrative, building on each others ideas.

☐ Help your child build eye contact to help him build confidence so they can communicate with others. You can help your child build eye contact by holding a contest between you two, the person who keeps the contact longer wins.

☐ Another example that would help improve eye contact in child is to place a label on your forehead. Advise your child to look straight at your forehead instead of looking at your eyes. This is a good exercise especially for shy children who have a hard time looking at someone's eyes.

☐ When you as a parent think of teaching your child good communication skills, the first thing you might think of is teaching him the importance of saying words like "hi, please, thank you, may I." These are excellent, but you also need to go further if you want your child to develop extraordinary social skills.

☐ Formal Classes: One of the best things you can do is take your child to formal Social Skills classes. The curriculum usually breaks down basic social situations into easy to learn, and easy to practice, lessons from how to have host behavior and ways to share the control of play, to how to pick and keep friends.

☐ Video: One of the best ways you can also do is demonstrating social skills through video. There are many videos out you can choose from, so try different ones until you find what your child likes the most.

Media

Media is another source that has a big influence on children. You need to use this medium to your advantage in order to develop positive habits in your child's life.

The good parent is the one who invests in whatever he has available to help himself and the society. There is no doubt that the media has some benefits. Therefore, let me give you some tips so you can use media to help your child:

1. Television is number one source of media and has powerful effects not only on your child, but on everyone. Television has good and bad programs; therefore, you need to be careful what you let your child watch.

You need to propel your child to watch beneficial and educational programs. You also might consider buying cartoons programming that are designed to educate children.

When your child grows and becomes in his teens, you need to propel him to watch educational programs as well. If you find him watching an unsuitable program, you need to communicate with him effectively and explain to him that it is not suitable to watch such programs. Again, you need to communicate with him in a diplomatic way; otherwise, he will think that you are trying to control him.

2. Another source that you need to pay attention to is the internet which has become prevalent in almost every house. Therefore, you need to watch your child when he is online and you need to know what websites he visits on a daily basis.

Since the internet has become an addiction to many folks, you need to show your child how he can exploit it in a beneficial way.

3. Radio has also become an important source that many individuals listen to especially while driving. Therefore, when you are driving with your children in the car, you need to listen to educational shows so they learn to do the same when they grow up.

4. Newspapers and magazines are another source that you need to pay attention to. Newspapers tend to have a lot of negative news; therefore, it is better to propel your child to read books instead so he gains long term benefits.

Chapter 18:

Good Friendships

Does your child have good friends? Is he able to choose good and honest children?

Making sure that your child has good friends is another thing you must do if you want to develop a positive and productive child. Friendship is an important part in your child's life. It fulfills a social need for him and allows him to form experiences. Therefore, having good friendships helps your child to become a positive person because people in general like to make positive friends and spend time together.

As a parent, you need to take the necessary time to explain to your child what makes a good friend as well as how to be a good friend. Explain to your child that sharing, helping each other, keeping a secret, politeness are all good attributes to look for in someone. Also make sure you explain to your child that gossiping, envy, mocking, and hatred are all bad qualities and that he should avoid other children who have these attributes.

Your child must understand that friendships are important so he can exchange experiences with his friends, have a good time, and learn from each other. The individual who tries to stay by himself all alone will suffer socially and will feel ostracized.

It is also worth mentioning that friends have a big impact on your child. Therefore, you need to make sure that your child is surrounded by positive and well-mannered children. To help your child develop good friendships, follow the powerful tips listed below:

1. Be a caring parent

Make sure that your child knows that you are on his side and that you are there to help him. Help your child believe he can differentiate between good and bad and help him build new relationships. When your child feels that you are on his side, he will be open to your suggestions and change.

2. Be supportive

Advise your child not to be overly competitive with his new friends. No one likes to have arrogant friends.

3. Invite his friends over

Inviting friends over to the house is a good way to strengthen the relationship between your child and his friends. Remember to have something in mind for the kids to do as young children tend to need directions.

4. Help your child

Help your child deal with any miscommunication that might arise as miscommunications are prevalent among kids. Again, make sure you help your child interpret any misunderstanding in a positive way.

Chapter 19:

Inculcate Positivity

5 Tips to Help your Child Lead A Positive Life

There are five essentials that you must do to help your child lead a positive life:

1. You need to help him develop good habits such as the ability to think positive and interpret situations in a pragmatic way.

2. You need to teach him at an early age the importance of reading like reading educational magazines and books.

3. You need to help your child discover his skills and what he is good at. Some children are good at giving speech. Some are good at writing fiction. Some are good at writing poetry. Some are good at the arts. Some are good at mathematics. Therefore, it is imperative that you help your child figure out what he is good at and help him enhance those skills.

4. You need to help your child to build correct relationships that are based on care and compassion. You need to ask yourself, "Am I building healthy relationships so my child can learn from me?" How is your relationship with your child? Do you two communicate? Are you two friends? Are you able to learn from him even if your child's experiences are limited?

5. Your child needs to have a good role model. It doesn't have to be you. It could be someone else like one of the prophets, Mahatma Gandhi, or anyone else that is successful and positive.

Reading

Educating your child is very important and if you want him to become a positive individual, make sure you follow the advice that you give him.

The years keep evolving very fast and if you don't make your child stay up with the current knowledge and inventions, he will miss on many important innovations. One of the best ways you can stay up to date with the current knowledge and studies is by becoming an avid reader.

Reading is very important for every one especially the positive individual. Since he will deal with many people, he needs to talk to them about different topics. If his knowledge is limited and keeps repeating the same kind of information every time, people will start to avoid him.

People in general like to have new information. This is why it is very imperative that you; as the parent to make sure reading become a habit of your child since early childhood.

The question you might be asking as the parent; "What can I do to improve my child's reading skills?"

1. Teach your child to read by expressing the words they read by using hand gestures, facial expressions, and eye movements. This is good for young children who are not effective at reading yet.

2. For children who are able to read, you need to follow up with them and teach them to enunciate correctly and give each letter its correct pronunciation.

3. You also need to teach them by practicing silent reading, so they can understand the text. Then you can move on to help them read out loud so you can correct their mistakes and errors.

4. You need to stop whenever the child comes across a new word and explain it to him. This is a great way of developing your child's vocabulary.

5. Help your child to express the meanings of the punctuations through voice and facial expression.

6. Read to your child every day as it increases his knowledge and enhances his vocabulary. Take 20 minutes from your busy day and start reading to your child small stories. Then as your child grows, you can move on to more complicated books.

7. Go to library

Make going to the library with your child a habit of yours from an early age. You can find a lot of books to choose from. All you need is a Library card and it is for free.

8. Cook a meal

Once a week, start to cook with your child using his favorite cooking book. Make sure that the cooking book that you get for your child has pictures and activities for him to do, so he enjoys it.

How to Make your Child Love School?

Parents from all walks of life want their children to succeed in school. However, many struggle to make their child love school and get high grades.

To help you with your quest on making your child love school, follow the below points:

1. You need to affirm to your child that he loves school. Repeat such statements in front of your child and in front of others as affirmation will help program his subconscious mind with what you are affirming.

2. You also can invite his friends over to your house so your child can spend some time with his classmates.

3. You can coordinate with the school to honor more students every semester and coordinate with the school officials that he participates in these honoring events.

4. You can coordinate a trip for your child and some of his class mates to go together to have some fun like going to the zoo, park, or museum.

5. You can set example by turning the TV off and start reading a book that you enjoy. By taking the time to read, you are setting an example for your child that reading is fun.

6. Join your child on school trips. When you participate in your child's school activities, you are showing your child that you care and value his education. In addition, if your child tends to be an introvert, you can help him out become more social.

7. Invest in school aids. There are many things you can buy such as flash cards, games, and other software that will help your child enjoy studying. Make learning fun and make sure you participate in the fun as well.

8. Use experiences from your daily life. For instance, you two can count pieces of fruits that you have in the plate or count the bananas or apples. This is good for younger kids and they will learn Math while playing at the same time.

9. Make school an important subject in your house. Ask your child about his day and what he has learned. Ask him about what classes he enjoyed the most and let him explain the reasons. When you show interest, your child will begin to feel more important and will begin to think of school as something fun.

more important and will begin to think of school as something fun.

10. You need to compliment your child's progress constantly. Many parents make the mistake by complaining to their child if he doesn't get full marks. Your job is to compliment your child's progress, not put him down.

These are some ideas that you can follow with your child in order to make him enjoy school. In return, your child will start doing his home-work without pressure or force from you.

Chapter 20:
How to Make your Child Succeed?

Every parent wants his child to be successful and productive when he grows up, but the question is what can you do to help him build the habits of success?

When your child succeeds at any given moment in life, this will propel him to accomplish more and become more ambitious. Your child will also begin to feel more confident of his capabilities. Therefore, it is imperative my dear reader that you look for the motives and the sources that help your child succeed.

Below are the main keys to success that you need to ingrain your child's personality:

1. Confidence

Confidence is the first key of success your child needs in order to succeed in life. You as the parent have a big role to play in enhancing your child's confidence and self-esteem.

Remind your child that he is a powerful creature and has unlimited power. When he does something good, give him a compliment and encourage him to do more.

Never call him detrimental names such as "stupid, idiot, failure, loser, or lazy." These kinds of statements propel him to feel depressed and he will begin to feel lack self-esteem.

2. Encouragement

Every child has great potential and power, but needs passion to be brought to life. Your child will not achieve great results without having this high energy.

Your child needs financial and personal motivation to go after his dreams. Instead of forcing your child to do something, it is better to use encouragement methods such as:

☐ Search for the strong points in your child

☐ Encourage your child to study by giving him examples of successful people.

☐ Give him gifts whenever he accomplishes an important task and succeeds at something.

☐ Respect your child's playing and free time.

☐ Do not talk badly about schools or teachers in front of him

Leadership

There are many different definitions for leadership according to various researchers. However, most researchers agree that leadership means to direct a group of people towards a goal through various kinds of skills that the leader possesses to reach a certain result.

The successful leader has many skills such as:

1. The ability to communicate and express his ideas to others as well as the ability to listen to others.

2. The ability to affect others positively.

3. The ability to make effective decisions at the right time. Making a decision has to be made in the correct time in order to be correct, otherwise, it will make things worse.

4. The ability to plan for what might happen in the future by having a backup plan if things don't go as planned.

5. The ability to manage time effectively. Time management is a needed skill that must be studied in order to manage life.

6. The ability to control your emotions and know how to deal with different kinds of people.

7. The ability to work as a team and collaborate together. Leadership is not a one man show; it is a group of efforts.

These skills and traits are crucial to have as a leader. Therefore, in order to help your child become a leader in the future, you need to do the followings:

1. Give the child a chance to express his thoughts and emotions. Many parents unfortunately try to put restrictions on their children and dictate what they should do.

2. Specify a specific time to sit with your child to talk about leadership through giving him stories and examples.

3. Give your child some basic leadership tasks such as organizing his bedroom, making his sandwich, cleaning the balcony etc...

4. Surround your child by true leaders.

5. Help your child to start making decisions from an early age.

6. Encourage your child on a daily basis to get out of his comfort zone and take on tasks that he is not very familiar with.

7. Help your child to improve his social skills and enunciation as true leaders need to be able to communicate effectively and clearly with others.

8. Encourage your child to participate in family discussions. Never mock his ideas or his point of views. Mocking your child will weaken his confidence in his capabilities and he will start to doubt himself.

9. Encourage your child to participate in leadership sports such as swimming and horseback riding.

10. Teach your child bravery and how to face fear. This can be done by giving him examples and helping him deal in real life situations.

Remind your child that leadership doesn't mean selfishness or controlling others. Leadership means respect for thyself and respect for others. Inform your child that leadership is about the ability to manage life in a positive matter and the ability to affect others in a beneficial way.

How to Develop a Creative Child

So you want to develop creativity in your child?

Creativity is not something hard to develop in your child, but it requires big and continuous effort. Every parent wants his child to be creative and productive and I'm sure you are no exception.

Can you enhance your child's capabilities? Can you enhance your child's skills and hobbies so he becomes creative?

The answer is "yes." According to various studies, environmental elements play an important role in developing a creative child. Your child doesn't have to be genius to be creative as creativity is available for everyone. You can as well help your child enhance his creativity.

The creative child is someone who is curious and loves to learn about different kinds of things. He usually looks at things and then asks "how" and "why?" In short, he tends to have many creative ideas.

One of the best stories that I've read about the relationship between parents and children comes from a woman who has a son who is 10 years old. The mother says that her son loves reading and learning.

Since early childhood, she has made sure to bring for him short books that are filled with colored cartoons and the alphabets so he can play and learn. Now, it has become a habit for him to read every day.

The mother goes on to mention that he also loves computers. He goes online to play games, watches shows on the internet, and knows how to maneuver through the computer. His computer knowledge has increased and he has become expert compared to the children of his age. He has become ambitious and likes to learn about different issues.

When she was asked about the secret to her child's passion for learning, reading, and exploring, she said, "It is all about dedication."

She has dedicated her time to him. They communicate well and bounce off ideas to each other.

He has made a planning grid in which he writes his plans for the week, the time he is going to read, play, and study.

When the mother was asked to give an advice to parents, she replied, "Encourage your child constantly and try to enhance yourself so your child can learn from you."

Now, my dear reader, are you willing to take the time to encourage your child? Are you willing to invest in enhancing yourself so your child can learn good habits from you?

Chapter 21:

Neuro Linguistic Programming Method

What Is Neuro-Linguistic Programming?

It sounds like something you'd find in a science fiction movie, or perhaps in a government research lab. But in reality, neuro-linguistic programming is a collection of simple techniques that you can use to help your child meet their goals and lead a healthy, productive life. Neuro-linguistic programming builds off of techniques that most people already naturally use in conversation, while adding in borrowed tricks from psychotherapy and communication science to help you and your child find success. So how does it all work?

Psychologists have known for some time now that the language we use actually affects the way our brains work. All of our thoughts and feelings are coded into language in our heads. We use language to not only communicate with others, but to communicate with ourselves. Therefore, the structure of your native language actually has a huge impact on the way you perceive the world around you; it's very difficult to come up with thoughts and feelings that your language has no means of describing. The idea that language shapes the way we think has been around since the late 18th century, and has come to be known as the Whorf Hypothesis.

Since the beginning, there has been strong evidence to support the Whorf hypothesis. Consider, for instance, the Zuni people of New Mexico. This Native American tribe does not have the same array of color terms that we do; they only recognize words for "light" and "dark". When Zuni-only speakers were asked to determine if two swatches of color were the same or different, they were largely unable to make a distinction. But after being taught more words for color, performance on the task markedly improved. Their struggles with color had nothing to do with their eyes, brains or genes – they all had working color vision. The only difference was language. When language provides us with the tools we need to make sense of the world around us, our perceptions can drastically change.

Neuro-linguistic programming takes advantage of the power of language, and uses it to make real changes in problematic thought patterns and perceptions. You will learn how to use language to isolate your child's inner goals and desires, and help him or her to find more constructive ways of reaching those goals. All children want the same things – things like love, acceptance by peers, and success at school – but neuro-linguistic programming can help children realize that their difficult behaviour is not getting them any closer to those goals.

Neuro-linguistic programming is based on the work of Richard Bandler and John Grinder, linguists and authors based in California. In the 1970s, they invented NLP as a therapeutic technique based on the work of Noam Chomsky and other respected linguists. The original NLP was based on 'modelling', or the idea that each individual has his or own set of strategies for thinking about the world. The goal of NLP was to identify and challenge those models to attain the desired result. Since Bandler and Grinder's original work, many practitioners have refined and added to the NLP toolkit, producing a sophisticated set of strategies that can handle even the most difficult of behavior problems.

There are three main components of neuro-linguistic program to keep in mind before attempting to begin a program of behavior modification with your child. The three pillars of NLP are:

Subjectivity. Our perceptions of the world are entirely subjective, and unique to each individual. Two people who experience the same event will walk away with very different subjective interpretations of what happened, and they will be affected in very different ways. If two people observe a mother yelling at her child in public, one person might perceive the event as an example of poor parenting and anger management, while the other person might empathize with the mother and relate to the stress she must be feeling. Although the two people witnessed the exact same event, they came away with very different subjective interpretations. This is also why one person might be traumatized by a stressful event, while another person might come through the same event unscathed. It's important to keep these subjective interpretations in mind when dealing with your child, as they probably remember shared experiences very differently than you do.

Consciousness. There are two parts to the human mind – the conscious and the unconscious mind. The conscious mind is the part that we actively have control over, while the unconscious mind lurks beneath the surface. The unconscious mind contains desires and subjective interpretations which the conscious mind is not aware of. Unconscious desires have an impact on conscious behaviour, and with effort, the conscious mind can have an influence on the patterns formed in the unconsciousness. Remember that when you use NLP, you are seeking to change not only the conscious mind, but the way the unconsciousness works as well.

Learning. Above all, the mind is a flexible thing. We are constantly learning and adjusting our perceptions of the world to accommodate new information. Every subjective experience, every thought pattern and every internal model of the world was acquired through learning, and with the right techniques, better thought and behaviour patterns can be learned. The mind has a near-endless capacity for learning, and by tapping into the power of language, we can control and direct that learning to create better habits.

Neuro-linguistic programming is based around the idea of modifying a person's models. The idea of models was first developed by Virginia Satir, a famously successful family therapist who used the idea of modelling to repair even the most hostile of family relationships. Models were then modified by Bandler and Grinder for the individual, in order to help a person achieve success. Simply put, models are like the computer programs of the mind; they incorporate information and tell us how to feel and behave in the course of certain stimuli. No two people have the exact same set of models. You might have models for walking, for cleaning your kitchen, and interacting with your partner. Models encompass everything we do in life. A grandmaster chess player has a model for chess playing that other people do not, and a parent has models for nurturing and child rearing that non-parents do not. To learn a desired skill or gain a desired personal trait, what we really must do is develop a model for that kind of behavior. Neuro-linguistic programming provides "shortcuts" that let us modify the models of ourselves or others quickly, leading to actual change.

There are three steps to successfully choosing and integrating a new model, and all of the techniques in this guide will touch on these three steps in some way or another. These are:

Step One: Observe the Model. The first step is to identify the model that is causing the problems. Models can be identified by the behavior they create. For instance, if your child is prone to throwing tantrums in public, you are probably dealing with a 'tantrum' model. What your child does is a direct result of the models that he or she has. Once you have identified the model that is causing problems, you have to delve deeper into how it works, and why your child has it. This can be done by asking careful questions of your child's unconscious. For this to work, your child should be in an extremely relaxed state. You are not asking your child to respond consciously, but unconsciously, answering based on feelings and impulses.

Remember, every model exists in order to attain some kind of goal. A walking model exists so that we can get places. A friendship model exists because we crave companionship. And even the most mal-adaptive of models – like bullying, or fire-setting – exists because the child is trying to attain some kind of positive goal. When you observe the model, you must not only observe what it is, but why it exists and how it attempts to meet its goal. Once you have done this, you can begin to come up with models that might better serve to meet your child's goals. If your child is throwing tantrums to get attention, you might come up with a better model to gain attention, such as one that involves social interaction, or striving for high achievement.

Step Two: Find the Differences. When you have the current model

I and the ideal model identified, you must search for the key components that make the 'idealized' model effective. If your goal is to help your child become a productive, high-achieving student, focus only on the elements that are absolutely crucial for becoming one. A high-achieving student might be inclined to get up early each morning, but is that really an essential characteristic for success? Or would it be better to focus on time management as a crucial skill. But identifying only the core traits for success, you avoid overwhelming your child with too many demands and expectations, and you will see positive results much faster. You should also ask your child questions about their current strategies, to determine what kind of outcomes they're getting, and how those outcomes differ from their goals. Doing this will help your child's unconscious to realize that his or her current methods are not useful, and should be changed.

Step Three: Design a Method. In order to see any real change in your child, the two of you should work together to come up with a set of concrete steps that your child will follow in order to see success. Your goal is to integrate the improved model into your child's existing one, or replace it all together. Your child should practice 'living' with the new model, by visualizing what it will be like to use the new strategies, and focusing on how it will feel to be a person with a different set of models. By closely monitoring your child's reactions during this stage, you can evaluate his or her progress and determine if he or she is receptive to change. Flexibility is important at this stage – your child will not stick to a method that he or she does not like, no matter how hard you try to program it into them. If you suggest that your child take up playing the trumpet as a way to combat boredom and your child resists the idea during NLP, he or she will be quick to abandon the instrument soon after the NLP is complete. NLP is a useful strategy, but it cannot work miracles – you must still be realistic when setting goals and coming up with strategies.

In this guide, you will learn several techniques for identifying, discussing and modifying your child's thought processes with nothing more than the power of language. These techniques can be applied to any child with reasonable verbal skills, regardless of their behavior problems. NLP can also be safely used alongside any other treatments or therapies your child is receiving. All you need is some patience, and a little bit of knowledge.

Chapter 22:

Approaching Your Child

Before attempting to use any therapeutic technique, it's important to establish a good rapport between therapist and client – or in this case, between parent and child. These techniques only work if your child feels comfortable enough to be honest with you about their inner thoughts and feelings, so it's important that you start by learning to have a productive conversation with your child.

If you have been dealing with difficult behavior from your child for a long time, it's natural to have tension and feelings of frustration between the two of you. Both you and your child may have come to expect that every conversation will turn to an argument. This is emotionally exhausting for the both of you, and ultimately counterproductive for applying NLP techniques. You must start by making a conscious effort to not lose patience with you child, and to keep a healthy conversation going. Since that is easier said than done, the following tips will help you to establish rapport with your child:

Be Non-Judgmental. One of the most important aspects of building rapport is to create a non-judgmental environment for your child to open up in. It is absolutely crucial that your child feels he can tell you anything without fear of negative consequences. Even subtle signs of disapproval – a disgusted facial expression, or a gentle chiding – can crush your child's trust, and prevent him from wanting to open up to you in the future. Even if your child confesses to misdeeds you weren't aware of, you must not react visually or verbally. Remember, punishing your child for wrongdoing is not working – it is much more important to get to the root of the problem. When trying to create a neutral, judgement-free environment, there are two things you must be aware of at all times: what's on your face, and what's coming out of your mouth.

Keeping a neutral facial expression and body posture is a skill that may take some practice before you attempt an intervention with our child. Our faces can often give away much more information than we intended, and even young children can read the nuances of a facial expression. Even a quick look of shock, anger or disgust can be enough to damage rapport with your child. Learn to keep a pleasant, neutral look on your face when speaking - you are there to listen and offer support, no matter what is said. Practice with a friend or partner, if you need to.

It is also extremely important to be mindful of phrasing when creating a non-judgmental environment. For instance, you must never ask your child a question that begins with the word 'why'. 'Why' questions automatically put a person on the defensive; they feel as if their actions are being criticized, and they are being forced to defend their decisions. Instead of asking your child a question like:

☐ Why did you hit that boy yesterday?

☐ Instead ask him:

☐ What were some of the reasons for hitting that boy?

☐ Can you tell me what led to you hitting that boy?

☐ What were some of the thoughts and feelings you had before you hit that boy?

Although these questions mean the same thing as 'Why did you hit that boy', the phrasing is much less confrontational. Instead of demanding an explanation, you are merely asking about the facts in a neutral, matter-of-fact tone. This technique will yield much better answers, without the moodiness or hysterics of a child on the defense.

Get on Their Level. It is crucial that you avoid patronizing, or 'talking down', to your child. Most children are far more intelligent than we give them credit for. You wouldn't appreciate it if your doctor treated you like a simpleton in conversation, and your child does not appreciate being talked down to either. Show him or her that their thoughts and feelings will be taken seriously by allowing them to have a serious conversation with you. Speak naturally, as you would to an adult.

Don't worry too much about using 'big' words on your child. Do your best to estimate your child's vocabulary, and give him or her plenty of chances to ask questions if he or she doesn't understand. Make sure to have your child repeat things back to you in their own words from time to time, just to be sure that they are following the conversation. You will probably be pleasantly surprised by how much they understand.

Rephrase. Kids, whatever developmental stage they are in can often express their emotions through confusing statements. This can be an extremely frustrating experience for both parent and child. To make sure that both of you are communicating effectively, you should rephrase the things your child is saying in your own words, to make sure you have correctly interpreted what they're trying to say. Doing this makes your child feel as though you are truly listening, and it gives them an opportunity to correct any misunderstandings right away. When done properly, this should look something like this:

☐ Child: When I go to class and see the teacher and everybody, I just get really mad sometimes.

☐ Parent: So I'm hearing that you get mad whenever you see your teacher, is that right?

☐ Child: No, not my teacher. It's just kind of everything, I guess. Just being at school in general. I like my teacher.

☐ Parent: Okay, I understand what you're saying now.

The child initially had difficulty expressing her feelings with words, but by rephrasing, the parent was able to clarify what she meant, and avoid having a conversation based on a misunderstanding.

Show That You Are Listening. Children spend a lot of time listening to adults, but they don't often feel as if their voices are truly heard. If you and your child have a history of heated arguments and verbal confrontations, they might be feeling like you just don't listen to them. It's important to correct this problem if you are going to use neuro-linguistic programming techniques successfully.

The proper signs of good listening are the same when speaking to children as they are when speaking to adults. Lean forward, toward your child, when he or she is speaking. Nod, and make small verbal cues such as "okay", "I see", or "that's interesting", to show them that you are paying attention. Using the same verbal cue over and over will eventually become monotonous, and have the opposite of the intended effect, so be sure to vary the things you say. Ask questions, and prompt your child to give you more information when necessary.

You should try to avoid fidgeting, or gesturing wildly when you speak. Some people have a habit of 'speaking with their hands', but for a child with attentional or behavioral deficits, all this gesturing can be very distracting. It also adds emphasis to what you are saying, and might make your child feel as if you are dominating the conversation. Keep your hands in your lap when you speak, or, if necessary, tuck them under your legs to prevent you from moving them.

Note that eye contact is not necessary to demonstrate to your child that you are listening to them. Many people are uncomfortable with long periods of direct eye contact, children in particular, and it may be easier for your child to speak freely if you do not make direct eye contact with him or her. Stare at a point on the floor or wall near your child, but don't look directly into his or her eyes unless you notice the child initiating eye contact first.

Use Open-Ended Questions. 'Closed questions' – that is, questions that seek a particular answer, like 'yes' or 'no', can be useful for establishing basic facts, but most of the time, you should try to use open-ended questions that require a thoughtful answer. If children can get away with provided minimal answers, they will choose to do so, and it will be much more difficult to have a conversation with your child. Some examples of closed-ended questions include:

☐ Did you feel angry when _____ happened?

☐ Did you hit your teacher?

☐ When did you get home from school?

These questions will help you learn essential information quickly, but you're not likely to get any detail or insight into your child's mind. When you need to probe deeper into the way your child is feeling, you should avoid closed-ended questions as much as possible. Instead, focus on open-ended questions that can be answered in many ways. Some examples of open-ended questions include:

☐ How did you feel when _____ happened?

☐ What was that fight like for you?

☐ What do you think of your new teacher?

Even a reluctant child is not able to dismiss these questions with a basic 'yes', or 'no'. Your child will be forced to give an answer with a little bit more detail, which can be used to keep the conversation going.

Know How to Use Silence. Silence can actually be a powerful tool in encouraging someone to speak freely about their feelings. From an early age, humans find long silences in conversation uncomfortable; our desire to avoid awkward silences is often greater than our desire to withhold information. If your child offers you a short or one-word answer, just wait. Maintain eye contact and stay silent, as if you are waiting for them to continue. After a few seconds, most people will elaborate on their answer, just to break the silence. Taking this pause also allows your child to gather their thoughts and more effectively express themselves, without feeling pressured for time.

Ask Them To Explain Their Feelings. Words like "anger" or "sadness" are a good start, but they don't always convey enough information. When your child tells you that they are feeling something, tell your child "Everyone experiences anger a little bit differently. Can you tell me what anger feels like for you?" Encourage your child to relay some of the thoughts that go through their mind when they feel this emotion, or some of the physical sensations they experience. Oftentimes, you may find that your child is actually trying to reference a more nuanced emotion, like contempt or envy, which they simply do not have the vocabulary to convey. Exploring your child's feelings a little deeper can help to prevent misunderstandings and lead to a richer conversation.

Normalize and Reassure. Children and adolescents often feel that no one else in the entire world is facing the same sorts of problems that they are. It goes without saying that it's extremely isolating to feel this way, and children and adolescents will often avoid discussing what they really feel, for fear that they might come across as 'odd' or 'strange'. When you notice your child being reluctant to speak up about an issue, normalize whatever it is they are going through by telling them they are not alone. You can phrase this in ways like:

☐ It's completely understandable. You know, a lot of people would have reacted the exact same way in that situation.

☐ Lots of kids your age have problems just like that. It's totally normal.

Problems can arise when your child is distressed about violence they have committed, or thought about committing. You will still want to offer reassurances to your child, but you must be careful not to normalize the violent behavior. Instead, focus on the emotions they are feeling, while still condemning the action. This can look like:

☐ Everyone is allowed to get angry from time to time, but no one deserves to be hit.

☐ I can understand why you got so angry yesterday, but it's never okay to hurt your sister.

By normalizing your child's feelings, but not their actions, you show them that what they are going through is normal and nothing to be ashamed of, but you do not reinforce unwanted behavior. This can be an extremely useful tactic for dealing with children who lash out due to some form of inner unhappiness.

If You Get Stuck, Don't Panic. Sometimes, you'll reach a lull in the conversation where you don't know what to say. Or your child may have a restless or difficult moment and become impossible to talk to. It happens. Don't worry. If you're stuck, don't be afraid to take a short break. Get a drink of water or a snack, or focus on another activity for a while. If you're honest with your child, you won't damage rapport. Use phrases like:

☐ You've really given me a lot to think about. I need a minute to process this.

☐ I think we've really made a lot of progress here. Why don't we stop and get something to eat?

☐ I really want to have this conversation with you, but we can't talk when you're like this. I'm going to give you some time to compose yourself, and then we can keep talking, okay?

Express to your child that you have hit a roadblock, and gently suggest that you continue the conversation some other time. It will be much easier for you, and much easier for your child.

From here on out, we will look at some crucial techniques in neuro-linguistic programming that will help you identify and change problematic patterns of thinking. Read each of the techniques carefully, and consider which ones you are most comfortable with, and which ones you think will work best for your child. If your first attempts don't work out the way you had hoped, don't discourage. Each child will respond to each technique in his or her own way, and it may take a few attempts before you stumble across the perfect technique.

Chapter 23:

Anchoring

Have you ever been walking down the street when a whiff of a familiar smell brought back a rush of unexpected happiness? Or heard an old song that reminded you of a long-forgotten crush? Have you ever felt a rush of anxiety as you drove past a place where something bad happened to you? If you have, then you are already familiar with the basis of anchoring.

'Anchoring' simply means that a particular emotional state can be 'anchored' to a certain stimulus, like a sound or a smell. These can be created gradually (for instance, you might come to associate the smell of freshly-baked cookies with the warmth and security of grandma after years of experiencing the two things together), or they can be created instantly (you probably instantly feel a rush of love and happiness every time you hear your wedding song). With this technique, you will learn to either identify existing anchors in your child's life, or deliberately create anchors to help your child achieve a certain mental state. Let's start by looking at a case study:

Eleven-year-old Patrick sometimes has difficulty focusing at school. At home, he has no problems completing his homework in the quiet of his bedroom, but at school, the noises and movements of his fellow classmates are sometimes too much for him to handle. His teacher complains that his is restless and does not pay attention in class.

How can Patrick's parents use anchoring to help their son?

In this case, we know that Patrick is capable of entering a state where he can concentrate on his studies. The key to helping him is to create an anchor that Patrick can use to enter that state outside of the house. Ideally, this should be something that Patrick can easily bring to school with him, so that he can create that some mental state in class.

After some consideration, Patrick's parents give him a stress ball to handle while he works on his homework. For weeks, Patrick is only allowed to hold the stress ball while he is focused on his homework; if his mind starts to wander, or if he does something else, he must put the stress ball down. At the same time, Patrick's parents encourage him to concentrate on his feelings of productivity and inner calm while he holds it.

After weeks of pairing the stress ball and his inner state of calm, Patrick's parents begin to allow him to use the stress ball outside of his bedroom. He continues to use it while he does homework, but he now practices taking it out, squeezing it, and settling into a state of concentration several times throughout the day. His parents monitor him closely, making sure that squeezing the stress ball is helping to summon the focused, concentrated state he has while doing homework. Eventually, he is able to bring the stress ball to school, and whenever he starts to feel distracted, he squeezes the ball and it helps him return to a focused state.

This example shows how an anchor can be easily created to help a child summon a desired mental state at will. Stress balls make ideal anchors, as most children are very tactile creates, and stress balls can easily be used at school, where problem behaviors often arise. Other anchors could include small pictures, scented items, or objects that make a particular sound. The key is to select an anchor that your child only encounters when he or she is in the desired mental state; if you choose something your child interacts with regularly, he or she will never form an association between the mental state and the anchor.

Chapter 24:

Reframing

Reframing is perhaps one of the most important techniques you will use in neuro-linguistic programming. Although it is not unique to NLP, its proven effectiveness has made it an essential part of many psychotherapy techniques; it is crucial to master reframing in order to have a successful intervention with your child.

If you've ever been told to "look on the bright side" or "find the silver lining", you are already familiar with the basic of reframing. Simply put, reframing means identifying the way your child perceives the world, and then helping your child change their perceptions in ways that are more positive or productive. We as human beings assign meaning to events, objects and people in our lives in order to make sense of the world, and those personal meanings change the way we think about and interact with the world around us. For instance, your child might view their school as a place where he or she is constantly being judged and attacked. To reframe this, you might guide your child into viewing their school as a place to learn wonderful new things and make new friends.

The first step to a successful use of reframing is to identify exactly what it is that your child wants. Every action we take has an underlying goal or intention, though it may not always be obvious what that goal is. Consider the following example:

Brendan is a fifth-grader who is frequently in trouble at school for bullying other children. His behavioural problems started in the third grade, and in the past two years, his parents have transferred him to three different elementary schools. Each time, the problems would begin again shortly after the transfer. Most recently, he was suspended for punching another child in the face. Brendan's parents are concerned that his bullying will continue beyond elementary school, and that they will eventually be forced to homeschool him. As a last-ditch effort, Brendan's desperate mother attempts to use neuro-linguistic programming to deal with her son's behavioural issues.

How could she use re-framing to deal with Brendan's problem?

At first, it might be tempting to claim that the underlying intention of Brendan's actions is to hurt other children, or to cause pain. This is not the case. Even the worst kinds of behaviour stem from good intentions. As humans, we strive for positive things – we want to be loved, we want to help our families, we want security, we want to succeed at work or school. Problems arise when an individual uses harmful and maladaptive strategies to strive for that goal. Brendan's goal here is not to harm other children; his bullying is just a technique that he has come to believe will help him achieve his aims. Specifically targeting Brendan's bullying is only going to put him on the defensive, as we'll see here:

Mother: Brendan, why do you pick on other kids at school?

Brendan: I don't know.

Mother: There must be a reason.

Brendan: I don't know, I just do.

Mother: You don't know why you're mean to other kids?

Brendan: No.

This approach looks like something a typical parent might try, and we can see right away that it has failed. Brendan's mother has not uncovered any useful information, and she's created more distance between herself and her son. By targeting her son's unwanted behaviour, instead of his general worldview, she puts him on the defensive; Brendan is being forced to explain something he may not yet know the answer to. By using a neuro-linguistic programming approach instead, Brendan's mother can get to the root of his problem and have a much more productive conversation.

Since it is the unconscious in Brendan's mind that is controlling both his bullying and his underlying intentions, Brendan's mother should seek to get in touch with her son's unconsciousness. There is an easy six-step program for successful reframing that she can follow to enact a positive change.

Step One: Identify the Problem. This part has already been done. Brendan's bullying behaviours are the problem that need to be changed, and that is what his mother hopes to achieve with her NLP.

Step Two: Establish Communication. This is where Brendan's mother must clearly specify that it is her son's unconscious mind, and not his conscious one, that she wishes to speak too. Brendan should be very relaxed before this step can begin. He should close his eyes, almost as if he is in a hypnotic state, and respond to questions with instinct alone. His mother should ask if the part of Brendan that bullies other children would be willing to communicate with her. The unconscious can be a very defensive place, so she should be careful to phrase her request as gently as possible. Brendan will feel some sort of sign when his unconscious is ready to communicate – this could be a bodily sensation, an image, a sound, or a general feeling of cooperativeness. When he feels it, he should let his mother know, and she will then proceed by thanking the unconsciousness for cooperating.

Step Three: Find the Good Intention.Remember, all problem behaviors arise from good intentions, even if it is difficult to see at first. Brendan's mother must keep this in mind as she moves to step three. She should ask the unconsciousness what its intentions are directly. This can be done with questions like:

What do you want?

What are you trying to do?

What is it you are trying to get?

If the child is reluctant or unable to answer, the parent should reaffirm that they are speaking with the subconscious, and reiterate that they are looking for the good in the child's actions. Brendan should be reassured that he will not get in trouble for his answer, and that this process will help him. The unconscious may provide vague answers at first; Brendan's mother should push the unconscious to clarify exactly what it wants so she will know how to proceed.

Step Four: Come Up With Alternatives. In this case, suppose that Brendan's subconscious admitted that he was bullying because he wants to be noticed by his peers. Brendan's bullying is not a desire in itself – it is merely a means to strive for the goal of being noticed. Since the bullying behavior is what needs to be stopped, Brendan should be asked to come up with three alternative strategies to gain attention from his peers. Not every subconscious will be able to come up with strategies on its own, and so Brendan's mother may need to make suggestions or otherwise assist with the brainstorming. Note that there is no need to analyze the suggestions in any way at this stage. In this case, Brendan and his mother might suggest that he replace his bullying by sitting with other students at lunch, joining the soccer team, and inviting his classmates to come over after school.

Step Five: Negotiation. This is the step where the suggestions from step four are analyzed. Brendan's mother must ask her son's unconsciousness if the three strategies are acceptable or not. She must ask his unconscious mind to think carefully about the suggestions. She should direct him to think about the consequences of each strategy. How much effort will it take? Will he enjoy it? Is he willing to try them out for a little while? Questions here must be direct, and thorough. The better Brendan's mother is able to convince his subconscious that these strategies are a good idea, the more likely he is to stick with them in the future and abandon his bullying ways.

If, however, the subconscious is unable to agree to any of the suggestions, the two of them should return to step four and come up with new strategies that are better suited to Brendan's liking.

Step Six: Envision the Future. It cannot be overstated how important it is for the unconscious to be convinced that the new strategies will be successful. This step requires a technique called Future Pacing, which will be explored later in this guide. In essence, Brendan's mother must direct her son's unconsciousness to envision what the future will be like if he implements the new strategies. He must imagine the first day of soccer practice, and what it will be like to kick the ball alongside boys his own age. He should envision sitting down at a table with his lunch and striking up a conversation with a fellow student. He should think about the things he and his classmates might like to do for fun at his house after school. Brendan's subconscious should be asked if these outcomes are better than the outcomes achieved by bullying. If the unconscious agrees that they are, then the unconscious must promise to abide by these strategies before allowing Brendan to re-gain conscious control.

If the unconscious ultimately decides it is not impressed by these strategies, Brendan's mother must return to step two to re-evaluate Brendan's goals and make sure she is clear on what he truly wants, and why the strategies may not help him attain them.

When using reframing, it is important to remember that your child's goals may not be something that you personally find fulfilling or worth-while. Especially in children with identified special needs, it may be difficult to understand where your child is coming from, or why seem-ingly trivial things are so important to him or her.

It's important to note that a child may be very skeptical of this process, particularly of bringing forth the subconscious to identify his or her intentions. Fortunately, a child's skepticism will not impact the results; the subconscious mind knows that what the parent is saying is true, and will respond accordingly.

Chapter 25:

Parts Integration

The unconscious mind is not always a unified force. When we experience a dramatic emotional upheaval or event, the unconscious mind can fracture into separate entities that feel differently about the event and its implications. These pieces are called Parts, and the formation of Parts is a normal experience that everyone will go through in their lives. One Part may want to react to a trauma by continuing on as if nothing happened, while another Part might prefer to react to the event with emotional displays. Problems can arise when two Parts come into direct conflict with one another. Their values clash within one mind, which can be an extremely uncomfortable experience that leads to the individual acting out. In order to correct this problem, we must learn to unify the two Parts that are at odds. Consider this example:

Fourteen-year-old Allison is chronically absent from school. On multiple occasions, she has been caught skipping class to hang out with her friends at a nearby mall or fast food restaurant. Her grades have begun to suffer. No matter how much her parents and teachers punish her, she continues to miss her classes. Lately, her parents caught her sneaking out at night, and they suspect that this was not the first time she'd snuck out.

How can her parents use Parts Integration to help Allison?

Like Reframing, Parts Integration involves a series of steps that seek to get in touch with Allison's subconscious. Unlike Reframing, however, this process will involve speaking to two separate parts of Allison's subconscious at the same time. This can be a tricky process, and these steps should be followed carefully:

Step One: Identify the Problem Behavior. Once again, we must being by firmly establishing the behavior we would like to change. In this case, the goal of the parts integration is to put an end to Allison's constant truancy. A successful intervention would mean her returning to a normal school attendance and ceasing to sneak out at night.

Step Two: Get in Touch with the Parts. Every problem behaviour is associated with two Parts — one part that wants to cease the behavior, and one part that wants to continue with it. This step involves contacting the Parts directly, which means that Allison will need to be very relaxed. Ideally, she should close her eyes and try to direct tension out of her body, so that she can focus solely on her mind. When her unconscious is ready to speak, it will give Allison a signal, which she should in turn relay to her parents. Her parent should confirm that they are speaking with the two parts in questions, and then they should direct Allison to envision holding the Parts, one in each hand. She may envision them however she pleases – as different colored flames, perhaps, or as two tiny people. Once she has made contact with the Parts and is envisioning them in the palms of her hands, she is ready to proceed.

Step Three: Speak to Part One. Like with Reframing, this technique is based on the idea that all behaviors are borne from good intensions. Allison's mother should address the first Part directly – in this case, she might begin by speaking to the Part that wishes to continue skipping school and sneaking out of the house. She should directly ask it what it wants, or what its intentions are. Do not be fooled by a negative answer; these Parts can be very resistant to change, and may try to deflect by offering a negative answer at first. There is always a positive intention buried in this Part, and continued questioning will bring it to the surface. In this case, the Part might concede that it wants to keep skipping school as a means of establishing independence. The behavior is therefore not entirely destructive, but an attempt to gain freedom.

Step Four: Speak to Part Two. Once the intentions of Part one have been established, the parent must make contact with the second Part to determine its intentions. Once again, questions should be clear and direct. The Part may initially present itself as simply being a contrast to Part one, but there is a hidden positive intention, and it will eventually be revealed with continued questioning. This answer will either be identical to, or compatible with, the intentions of the first Part. In this case, the Part of Allison that wishes to stop skipping school might admit that its intentions are to regain the trust of her parents and teachers.

Step Five: Reintegrate. When both intentions have been established, the parent should address both parts at once. She must show the two parts that their aims are really the same, and they have no need to conflict with one another. Allison's mother could explain to the parts that what they both really want is to live as an independent, confident young woman, and the only way to do that is to gain the trust of the authority figures in Allison's life. The two parts can both get what they want at the same time; if Allison stops cutting classes, she will regain the trust of her parents, who will be more willing to grant her privileges. One this has been explained, Allison must merge the two Parts together. She should do this by slowly moving her hands together, while envisioning the images of the two parts blending together into a single, unified whole. She should then slowly press her hands to her chest, and envision the new, single Part returning to her body. She is now fully reintegrated.

Step Six: Consider the Future. Allison's conscious mind should take a moment to reflect on the reintegration; she should be asked about how she feels, and what feels different. She and her mother should also discuss how this reintegrated self will behave in the future, and how this process will affect her decisions.

Whenever Allison feels her behavior beginning to change again, she can repeat this process by herself by reminding herself of the two Parts, their matching intentions, and melding the individual visualizations in her hands before returning them to her body.

Chapter 26:
Visual/Kinesthetic Disassociation

Sometimes, a child's difficulties are the direct result of trauma. In these cases, Reframing and Parts integration will not help; the only solution is to help the child ease the pain of the trauma. Visual/Kinetic Disassociation (VKD) is a powerful technique that can help children and adults quickly recover from symptoms associated with PTSD. VKD allows sufferers to numb the pain of their memories by reliving them over and over while relaxing in a safe environment. Consider the following example:

Ten-year-old Dylan is living with his single mother, after a traumatic incident involving his father. Dylan's father had come home drunk and angry one evening, and had beaten Dylan and his mother. Police were called to the home, and Dylan's father was arrested. Since that night, Dylan has become withdrawn and fearful. His performance in school is suffering, and he has become socially withdrawn. He wakes screaming from nightmares, and lashes out angrily at school.

How can Visual/Kinetic Disassociation be used to help Dylan recover?

To start with, Dylan's mother must set up a safe, calming environment in which to perform VKD. There should be comfortable seating, like a couch or easy chair, available for Dylan. If possible, there should also be low, soothing lighting. The room should be silent, or contain nothing but gentle background music with no lyrics. The overall atmosphere should be one of utmost calm and safety.

Once Dylan is settled in to this environment, his mother can begin with VKD. To start, Dylan should recount the traumatic events that are causing him distress. He does not have to go into detail if he finds that he is not able to, but he should at least give a brief outline of the incident. His mother should closely monitor his reactions, to make sure that the exercise is not too intense for him. If he becomes overwhelmed, she can stop the session to give Dylan a break before continuing.

After giving his initial account of the story, Dylan will be very upset and emotional. The VKD session cannot continue until he has returned to a calm state. This can be achieved by quickly changing the subject to a happier topic, or by allowing Dylan to take a break and walk around the house to ease his anxiety. When he is ready to continue, his mother should start by ensuring that he is extremely relaxed. One easy way to do this is with the 'high tide' exercise – Dylan should close his eyes and imaging that he's standing on a beach, watching the tide roll in. Each time the tide comes in, it comes up a little higher, and when it washes out again, it takes all of his tension with it. Relaxation should start from the feet and work upwards as the water works its way up his legs, up his torso, and finally to his head. Dylan's mother may direct this exercise, or she can allow Dylan to visualize it on his own.

When Dylan is completely relaxed, it is time to start the technique. His mother should start by instructing him to call up the painful memory in his mind's eye. He must start the memory at the beginning, at the very last moment he was safe – in this case, right before his father came home. In his mind, Dylan should imagine that he's in a movie theatre, watching the memory play as a movie up on the big screen. Visualizing this way adds a layer of dissociation to the memory, which is crucial for VKD. The goal is to disassociate the memory from traumatic feelings by replaying it over and over again in a safe environment, until it ceases to be an emotional trigger and merely becomes just another memory.

When Dylan has visualized his mental movie theatre and selected the first frame, he should play through the memory in his mind from start to end, just like a movie. The memory should end once Dylan is safe again – in this case, when the cops have taken his father away. When he is finished replaying the movie, Dylan will be very upset, and it is crucial that he reach a state of calm once more before attempting to replay it again.

This process should continue until Dylan's aversive reactions to the memory aren't as strong. Each time should be the same – he pictures the theatre, watches the movie, and then calms himself down, reminding himself that he is safe. Eventually, the constant pairing of a safe environment and a traumatic memory will reprogram his brain to erase the threat from the memory. It will always be an unpleasant memory, but Dylan should be able to call upon it without experiencing severe distress. VKD does not have to be completed in a single session – it may take multiple attempts before the memory of a truly traumatic event can begin to dull. The key is patience – this technique has helped thousands of soldiers and civilians around the world recover from PTSD and other traumas, and bring the joy back into a shattered child.

Chapter 27:

Swish Patterns

While many of the techniques described here are used to improve a child's overall outlook and disposition, swish patterns are used to specifically target an unwanted habit. A swish pattern is a simple trick that can be easily set up to stop a bad habit in its tracks. Swish patterns work by teaching a person to mentally switch from focusing on their bad habit, to focusing on a goal that can only be achieved by conquering the bad habit. Practice this association until it is automatic; this will make it much, much easier for your child to summon the willpower needed to break his or her bad habit. Consider the following example:

Mia constantly bites her nails. Lately, her nail-chewing has gotten so bad, she has bitten her nails until they began to bleed. Mia's parents are concerned, and they would like to put an end to her habit.

How can Mia's parents use swish patterns to end her nail-biting?

The first step is to identify a visual 'cue' – remember, this should be something that Mia will see every time she goes to bite her nails. In this case, that might be the image of her fingernail moving toward her mouth. Whenever she sees or imagines this image, we want Mia's mind to switch to visualizing something positive – for her that might be an image of healthy fingernails with pretty nail polish on.

In the early stages, this pairing can be visual. Mia's parents might have her bring her fingernails up to her mouth, and then immediately stare at a picture of healthy, manicured nails. Repeat this over and over again, using pictures of healthy nails that Mia finds appealing. When an association begins to form, Mia's parents ask Mia to begin doing this mentally. They have her bring her fingers to her mouth, and then ask her to mentally summon an image of healthy, pretty nails. It is crucial that Mia learns to do this in her head, since she won't have actual pictures of nail polish available every time she feels like biting her nails. Mia's parents repeat the pairing over and over again, each time asking Mia to mentally imagine a set of lovely fingernails.

After hundreds of repetitions pairing the image of her approaching fingernails with images of the nails she desires, Mia forms an automatic association between the two. Each time she raises her hand to bite her nails, her mind brings up images of the ideal nails, and she is able to find the willpower to not bite her nails. Her parents monitor her carefully through all of this, and are quick to remind her of her visualizations every time they catch her bringing her fingers to her mouth.

Chapter 28:

Future Pacing

Evaluating progress after the application of methods is a necessary step; when using neuro-linguistic programming, we do that with a technique called Future Pacing.

Our brains are wonderfully complex organs, and one of the side-effects of having such a complicated brain is that it has difficulty distinguishing imagined situations from reality. If, for instance, you imagine yourself falling from a cliff, you'll find that your heart rate will increase, saliva production will decrease, and your sweat glands will start to work a little harder. Your body will go through the physical reactions you'd experience if you were really falling, even though the situation is entirely in your head and you were never in any real danger. We can use this to our advantage to create positive change, and help our children prepare themselves for future challenges.

In Future Pacing, we can check someone's progress by having them mentally walk through the perceived outcome of the future before and after an NLP intervention and monitoring the physical reactions. If there is a marked change in reaction, we can be confident that the NLP technique is creating progress. Consider the following scenario:

Thirteen-year-old Noah has been struggling in school. He's a quick learner, and he has a good grasp of the material, but he's not able to keep up in school. He frequently hands his assignments in late, or completely forgets to complete them. He takes poor notes in class, and permissions slips never seem to make it home in his backpack. His mother used NLP to discover that Noah's intention is to make sure his parents are never disappointed in him, and he has been choosing to do that by lowering their expectations of him. During a Reframing, Noah promised to start taking his schoolwork seriously and stop missing deadlines. His parents want to make sure those strategies will work for him.

How can they use Future Pacing to predict what their son will do?

Once again, this is a technique that requires Noah to relax. His parents should make sure he is comfortably settled in, and that he releases any muscle tension. Prior to the NLP, when asked about the future, Noah would become restless and unsettled, with a faster pulse and strange inflections in his voice. To check and see if their intervention has made any progress, they will need to compare his reactions after NLP with his reactions from before.

Four possible future outcomes must be decided on for Noah. These outcomes should be plausible and reasonable – for instance, Noah might envision completing an essay on time, or being well-prepared for a test. Once an outcome has been chosen, Noah must walk through it in his mind. This should be a very thorough walkthrough, and not a passing fantasy. He should begin somewhere early in the 'scene' – perhaps at the front doors of the school as he arrives to hand in his essay. The sights, sounds and smells around him must match the ones he would actually see in the real-life situation, and he should take his time to imagine all of them. The entire outcome must be envisioned, step by step. He should watch himself walk through the doors, down the hallways, and turn into his classroom. He should envision the faces of his classmates, the noise of the school bell, and the way that the paper feels in his hand as he turns it over to the teachers.

When he has reached the end of his imagined scenario, he must take the time to reflect on the experience. In particular, he should focus on the various emotions he felt as he lived the scene – in this case, a mixture of happiness, pride and relief. He should also consider whether the outcome is something he deems desirable, and if he wants to go through with making that vision a reality. He must decide if he is willing to make that change, on a conscious and unconscious level.

Once he has agreed to a particular strategy, he must consider it further, and look for ways that it can be fine-tuned for maximum success. Remember, the more agreeable the strategy is to him, the more likely it is that he will be able to stick with it and find success. For instance, in this case, Noah might agree that he is comfortable seeing a tutor to help get him caught up on his studies, but he might decide that he's more comfortable hiring a local college student as a tutor, rather than an older student from his own school. Allowing your child to make small adjustments will also help them to feel that they are making valuable contributions to their own future, which means they will be more invested in the outcome than if they are simply told what to do.

These visualizations must be repeated for all four strategies. It is not necessary for the child to agree to all four of the strategies – the parent can decide how many the child should agree to before they can move on. It may be that one is sufficient, or the parent may feel more comfortable having one or two more as "backups". If the child does not agree to enough strategies, simply return to the brainstorming stage and come up with more, before repeating the visualization task.

When the strategies have been finalized, the child should be asked to visualize him or herself in the future, after the strategies have been applied. In Noah's case, he should envision himself later on in the school year, where he is successfully caught up on schoolwork and maintaining good grades. He should imagine what it will feel like to be that person, and how other people will respond to him differently than they currently do. Ideally, this should be a positive experience for him. His parents should watch closely for his physical reactions – his breathing, his posture and his movements. They should also ask him to speak about what he is feeling, and judge the tone of his voice and choice of words. If the NLP has been successful, Noah should appear to be much calmer and more confident than he was at the start of the session.

Future Pacing can be used throughout a course of NLP to judge a child's progress. Ideally, a visualization should be done at the start of every course of programming, and the child's physical reactions should be judged. If a child with difficulties is asked to imagine how his life would be if he continues on its current path, you will likely see him breathing quickly, tensing up, and speaking in tones of panic, frustration or apathy. After the NLP treatment is complete, the Future Pacing task is used to check the child's progress. If the child does not appear to have made significant progress, then the NLP can be repeated at a later date, or a different method may be selected. As mentioned earlier, the mind is a subjective thing, and no two children will respond the exact same way to neuro-linguistic programming.

Chapter 29:

How to Improve Your Bond with Your Child

Creating a strong connection with your child is one of the most essential aspects you being a good parent. It's something every mom must do, and it is what's needed in order for a happy relationship. Many moms might think they know how to do this, but sometimes it can be hard for them. This chapter will go over how to improve the bond between your child and you, and some of the things you can do to make it better.

1. Being Involved in Their Life

A common problem with many children is they might say their parents aren't really involved. If you're a very busy parent, hiring babysitters to watch over your child is a must! However, you need to be present in his life. It does take time, and sometimes you have to sacrifice things, but you have to be there for them. If they have a problem, listen to them. If you feel like they need a friend, then get involved in their life. You can even help them with their homework they may get, and it will help improve not only their learning ability, but also the connection that you have with them.

2. Talk to Them

One way to form a better bond with a child is to talk to them. A child isn't some sort of alien species, but rather a child is a person, just like you. They have ideas, feelings, everything in between. You should talk to them and get to know them. You can even ask them every day how they're doing, and if they need help, you can rectify any situations that might come up. It does take time and perseverance, but the results are worth it.

3. Be Consistent

One thing you must do is establish consistency. Not only with punishment, but more importantly, your reward system. If your child notices that you are only consistent with your punishments and not with your rewards, he will resent you. If you have a nightly ritual, keep it in, and this will show your child that they can trust you, and you'll seem like an even better mom because of it. Having a mom that they can trust goes a long way, so it's imperative that you make sure you're consistent as well with your child in order to create a better, more fulfilling relationship.

4. Listen to Them

Just because you are a parent, doesn't mean that you're a tyrannical ruler. What you need to learn is to listen to them, and get to know what's going on. If you have a fight, listen to their side of the story. If they want to tell you something, let them. Even if it's something that you don't understand, being able to at least talk with them can build trust, and later on, that trust ca do a whole lot of good later on. If your child has an issue when they get older, they will go to you for advice instead of some other person that you might not approve of. So yes, listen to them and care about what they say. It's important

5. Establish Time Alone with Your Child

A mother does need to have alone time with a kid. It's nice to have the entire family together, but you need to spend quality time with them. If you have a daughter, maybe take them out shopping or to get their nails done. If you have a boy, maybe go to the toy store or to something that he might enjoy. Just take them out and spend some time with them every once in a while. That bonding time can do a whole lot of good later on.

6. Respect Them

A child isn't someone that you should just boss around all the time. You have to respect your child and be friendly with them. Talk with them in a polite manner and learn what issues they're coming across. You need to respect your child just like he was an adult. This not only improves the bond with your child, but it does something else as well. It establishes the valuable lesson that a child must respect others in life. It's a valuable lesson to learn, and one that many parents need to instill in their child.

Chapter 30:

How to Bring Happiness Back to Your Home

Figuring out the root of explosive behavior

Meltdowns and tantrums are particularly concerning as they happen more intensely, more often, or past the age where they are expected developmentally—those terrible 2's up through pre-school. As your child ages, aggression will become increasingly harmful to the child and you. Plus, it may become a huge issue for him with friends and at school, as well.

If your youngster consistently lashes out it might be because of an underlying issue that requires treatment. A few possible reasons for a child's aggressive behavior includes:

ADHD: Children who have ADHD are easily frustrated, particularly in specific situations, like when they are supposed to go to bed or do homework.

Anxiety: Anxious children might keep his anxieties secret, and lash out as the demands at home or at school place pressure on him that he cannot handle. Oftentimes, a toddler who "keeps it together" in school will lose it with a parent.

Learning disability that is undiagnosed: As your youngster repeatedly acts out during homework time or in school, it might be because the work is difficult for him.

Sensory processing problems: Some toddlers experience trouble in processing the data they're taking in through the senses. Things such as crowds, too much noise, and "scratchy" clothing may make them overwhelmed, uncomfortable, and anxious. It may produce actions which leave you mystified, which includes aggression.

Autism: Kids on every point of the spectrum often are susceptible to huge meltdowns as they're frustrated or experience unexpected change. Also, they oftentimes have sensory problems which make them agitated and anxious.

Given that there are so many potential causes for extreme emotional and aggressive behavior in children, an accurate diagnosis is critical to obtaining the appropriate assistance. You might want to begin with your pediatrician. He or she may rule out any medical causes and refer you to a trusted specialist. An experienced trained child psychiatrist or psychologist may help in determining what underlying problems are present.

Chapter 31:

Be still

If you play with well-used tennis balls you would find it is easy enough to tell one from another when you hold it in your hand. However, put it into play and all balls look much the same for you cannot see the telltale identifying marks and scuffs.

The same thing happens in life. When we get involved in the hurly-burly drama of doing this and that, there is so much going on our attention is all 'out there' and it is only when we stop and 'collect our thoughts' that we see the details.

Eckhart Tolle says, 'When you lose touch with inner stillness, you lose touch with yourself. When you lose touch with yourself, you lose yourself in the world.'

Like a game of tennis, the ball is lobbed to us and we leap to respond by attacking, defending or picking up the ball.

To see what is truly going on we need to get to a place of still-ness.

I mentored a mother who had a personality clash with her middle son. Everything he did annoyed her. She was recently divorced and had moved in with a new partner. Her son's insecurity made his behavior even more intolerable to her. In her first session with me the only emo-tions she could identify were anger and guilt. She left with a notebook and instructions to just observe the interactions she had with her son and note down any emotions she felt. When she came back the fol-lowing week, she noted her emotions as anger, guilt and frustration. The following week she noted down anger, guilt, frustration and hope. Happily, at the end of the mentoring program she had advanced to feeling other emotions such as love, peace, acceptance and joy.

When we are still we can fully see, hear and use all our senses to ob-serve the motion and dynamics of what is really going on. This is what is meant by the phrase being 'present'.

Stillness sounds easy but it is deceiving. It is when we are still we get a sense of what is wrong. Sometimes when we are still we start to feel the pain of our existence or situation... How often do we encourage people who are grieving to make themselves busy to 'take their mind off things'?

'Busy' becomes a lifestyle and as a parent you are always busy. In fact, to not be busy takes some planning and application, which is hard to commit to if you have a nagging suspicion that pain and other unsettling feelings will come to the surface if you take a few moments to yourself. The truth is, it is far easier to keep busy and leave those underlying feelings unaddressed.

Taking the time to be still is necessary for us to see what is really going on. Until we can see the dynamics at work we cannot know what needs to change.

Chapter 32:
Setting Out Your Limit

Take a look at the following scenarios:

☐ Parent: "Sally, you can watch cartoons after you pick up your clothes from the bathroom floor."

☐ Parent: "Terrie, you can go outside after you finish your math homework."

☐ Parent: "Tanisha, you can invite your friends for a sleep-over this weekend only after you clean up your room. It's up to you."

The above scenarios are few examples of appropriate limit setting by parents.

Setting limits not only teaches children responsibilities but also teaches them to follow rules and to respect adults. Inevitably, children will test the limits. When a parent sets such limits, the youngster learns that he has the power to earn or to lose an incentive, that his behavior leads to consequences, and that he has the power to create the outcomes he desires. This empowers the child and assists him in increasing his self-esteem. It teaches him that he is a part of the family and that he can make meaningful contributions. Parents may get frustrated, especially during a time when a child leaves a mess behind in his room and throughout the house. Some parents go ahead and clean it up while others, who are more sensible to the child's developing sense of responsibility, encourage the child to do so. Of course, children do not always do it happily and many try to engage in a power struggle with the parent. That is when knowing how to set limits and remaining consistent comes into play. If you tell your child something like, "Well, it's too nice outside so you can clean your room after you come back from your soccer practice," he may get the message that procrastination is acceptable or that undesirable behaviors do not necessarily lead to consequence. In turn, he will try to elicit a response from you that is beneficial for him each time. After all, if it has worked once, why should it not work for him again and again?

Some parents will try to justify their own disciplining methods at a later time and may provide excuses as to why they redirected the child to do something. The following are some examples:

"I did not want to argue with him."

"I thought that she'll think I wasn't fair."

"I wanted him to have fun."

"I want him to think that I am a good mother." In addition, these parents may try to over-correct their own behavior afterwards. At times, they may set limits that are either age inappropriate or set a limit but do not carry through with what they expect of the child.

Time Out

In order for a child to learn what their limitations are, parents need to set limits that are clear, doable and appropriate to each situation and to the child's age. You have to be consistent If Mom does not carry through with the limits she sets, how is the child supposed to learn what is acceptable and unacceptable? Why should the child listen and do what the mother had asked?

When a child is in time out and tries to engage the parent by either talking or acting out, the parent should avoid engaging the child before the time out is over. A good suggestion is to use a cooking timer or a large clock that the child can read to show to him when time out is over. For example the parent can say, "Johnny, you have ten minutes,"and explain to him ahead of time, "If you talk before the timer goes off, I will restart your time." This means that if the time out is broken, the clock timer will be re-set. Too often parents become frustrated and do not carry through with their original expectation. In return, the child will win in this situation and will continue to act out in the future, knowing that the parent will give in sooner or later. A general rule when placing a child in time out is to allow the child to remain in it for a minute for each year of his age.

For example, it is unreasonable to place a four-year-old child in time out for twenty minutes or a twelve-year-old child in time out for five minutes. Setting limits is not enough. In order for them to be effective, they must be age appropriateand reinforced immediately after the misbehavior has occurred and used on a consistent basis. It is not necessary for a child to be totally still and completely quiet while in time out. Some impulsive children will find this task too difficult. What constitutes a time out is when a child is removed from the environment in a special area like a chair, sitting on the sofa or somewhere where he cannot participate in activities such as playing, watching TV, or interacting with others. It is then expected that the child sit in this area for his time out. Some children may yell, cry, fidget, or stand up while others remain quiet and composed. This is all acceptable as long as the child does not leave the area that is used as his time out place. A parent can decide and inform the child that coming out of the area (an imaginary line can be used for older children or a visible marker of some sort for younger ones) will constitute breaking the time out. At this time, the parent can reset the timer and ask the child to return to the time out area. If a child repetitively breaks his time out after five consecutive times, the parent then can resort to sending the child to his room or use another consequence at that time. The parent should not tell the child the he or she has five chances but inform the child that if time out is not followed, another stricter rule will follow up as a result.

For instance, if it is closer to bedtime and Billy was expecting to watch his favorite evening program after his time out but was not able to complete his time out, he may be sent to bed early. A consequence will differ from child to child, and the parent will need to use his best judgment based on the situation at hand and what the child knows to be a reward and a consequence. For example, if a child likes solitary activities, the parent will not send such a child to his room☐that would be a reward. Instead, the child may be assigned house chores. As a parent, you will know what your child likes and dislikes and can assert your best judgment as to how to consequent undesirable behavior and reward desirable behavior.

Some children require longer to actually grasp the idea of what is expected of them. This all depends on their age and developmental abilities. The parent may want to resort to time out again the following day if the child misbehaves. In order for time out to work, parents need to be consistent. Time out may not work the first time around, but when used appropriately and immediately following the misbehavior, the child will become familiarized with it as a form of a consequence. For instance, if the parent finds out that the child had misbehaved at school, placing the child in time out will not be appropriate when the child returns home hours later. In such a case, another consequence needs to be implemented.

For example, if the child was expecting to go out and play outside after school, the consequence that the parent may use is not allowing the child to go outside. Of course, a parent must remember not only to give consequences but also to create opportunities for the child to correct his behavior and earn back privileges. This leads to a healthy balance and not only teaches the child autonomy but also that his actions lead to desirable or undesirable outcomes and that he has the power to change his behavior.

Reasonable vs. Unreasonable Expectations

When a parent changes his expectations of the child, something great happens☐there is a change in the outcome of behavior. Parents who are sensitive to the needs of their child are prone to having more reasonable expectations than those who merely react to their child's behavior. Expectations that are clear and age appropriate are those that will most likely be met by the child. On the other hand, expectations that are either too high or age inappropriate will be unmet. You have to remember that children will remember inconsistencies and persistence. For example, a parent who is allowing her twelve-year-old daughter to do her own laundry but fights with her to have her load the dishwasher is not having realistic expectations of the daughter. A father who expects his five-year-old son to do his baby sister's laundry in addition to cleaning the bathroom every evening is expecting a bit too much from the child.

At times, parents who have not been actively present in the child's life☐for example, if the child was raised by extended family members, came from a foster home, or was raised primarily by the sole custodian or guardian☐face issues they must address, and they may lack the tools to parent effectively.

This may be a common occurrence in situations where the child has suffered an illness for a prolonged period of time. It is not unusual for parents to try and rescue the child by trying to meet each of his needs. This is not helpful to the child because it does not allow him to develop a sense of age-appropriate autonomy and responsibility. In the long run, the parent will feel frustrated when the child does not meet the set expectations, and the parent will continue to do injustice to the youngster. An example is the case of the twelve-year-old girl from whom the parent expects only the minimum. In that scenario the daughter may grow up to be overly dependent on others and irresponsible. Correcting behaviors early in the child's development is important in ensuring that the child develops moral and ethical healthy character. Children should be able to participate in family life by having on-going age-appropriate responsibilities.

Avoid Sending Mixed Messages to Children

It is best for parents to give clear messages to the child. Some examples of mixed messages are:

Parent: "Timmy, I am glad that you won second place. Johnny must have worked harder, though, to get first place."What the child hears is, "You're good but not good enough."

Parent: "Sally, why can't you clean up after yourself like Jenny does?" What she hears is, "You may not be capable of cleaning your room or you're not as smart as Jenny in remembering to clean up after yourself."

Parent: "Tyrice, what is the matter with you? Why did you get another F?" The child hears, "There must be something wrong with you to get another F," or "You're not really smart since you gets Fs."

In order to discipline sensibly, a parent needs to evaluate how the child may interpret the message that he hears. Constant negative feedback will ruin a child's self- esteem and his desire to keep on trying. Therefore, do your best to avoid this. After all, if his efforts are not acknowledged and he is not encouraged, why not just give up? He may think that if his mom an dad do not think he is good enough, why bother? Instead, a parent can find a positive trait in a child, focus on it, and encourage its development. Too often, parents focus on the things their child is not yet capable of doing instead of exploring what things he may be really good at and fostering those skills and traits. Not every child will be a baseball player or a famous ballerina or be good at math. Just as adults have different occupations in life; children have their own unique place in childhood. Each child learns from trial and error, but no child will be inspired to learn new things and skills if he hears only criticism and ridicule. Children will usually try to please those adults to whom they look up and this often starts with their parents.

Kids are like little sponges. They are not only observant of their environment, they are also able to remember and use information according to their developmental level. The more positive and straightforward feedback a parent can offer to a child, the more the child will strive to perform and develop his talents. In most cases, positive attention and positive reinforcement bring about a positive behavioral change in a child.

When setting a consequence a parent needs to be clear about his expectations. A parent who gives a child the opportunity to earn a privilege or earn trust back must not break his promise. It is imperative that when you do make promises to your child, you have to follow through. There is nothing more discouraging to a child who tries to correct his behavior than to fail to receive an acknowledgement from his parents.

Privileges vs. Rewards

There is a difference between allowing a child to earn a privilege and rewarding him. Children expect rewards while privileges are earned. Rewards are spur of the moment while privileges are clearly defined.

For instance:

Parent: "Molly, you may not use my blow drier today. You forgot to put it away after using it yesterday. You can use it tomorrow, and I expect you to remember to put it away when you're done."

Parent: "Charlie, I'm sorry but you cannot stay up an extra half hour to watch TV tonight because you were late to school this morning.

When you show me that you can set your clock on time and get ready for school instead of being late, we can discuss letting you stay up again." Do you recall the difference between a reactive and a sensible parent?

A reactive parent who uses rewards as a way of disciplining a child may tell the child something like this:

"Molly, if you do your chores, I'll give you a dollar."

"Tommy, if you're a good boy at the store, I'll buy you an ice-cream."

"Tyrice, if you do your homework, I'll let you watch TV late."

"Billy, if you pick up your laundry from the bathroom floor, I'll let you play outside."

Do you notice a pattern in these scenarios? A parent who uses rewards in order to elicit a desirable behavior in a child uses the if-then pattern (if you do "this," I will do "that" for you). Unfortunately this pattern will work only temporarily. There will be times when the parent will not be able to follow through on his promises or will be unwilling to do so for fear of being taken advantage of.

The difference between a parent who uses privileges and the one who uses rewards is that the latter does so and expects the child to display a desirable behavior. This parent uses means such as modeling and encouragement and does not overuse rewards because he knows that the child will comply only as long as he can provide. The sensible parent explains to the child that acting appropriately is necessary, not just to get something right away but just for the sake of doing well. In the long run, the parent teaches the child patience, self-control, and responsibility. A child who learns these qualities will be proud of his performance and will strive to do well because, in time, this will become part of his personality. A parent who uses rewards over and over to elicit a desirable behavior will raise a child who will be overly dependent on others and who will be discouraged from trying to do well if there is no immediate reward at the end.

Children who see that their desirable behavior is acknowledged and valued at home develop a higher sense of belonging and responsibility within the family unit and will most likely continue to strive to do well. This will manifest through specific achievements in their lives.

Creating an Incentive System

As an incentive for positive behavior, implementing an incentive system will help strengthen the behaviors that you want to reinforce in the child. An easy system to create is one in which the child earns daily tokens such as stickers, marbles, or plastic chips which can then be used to "purchase" or "redeem" a special age-appropriate incentive such as extra time to watch TV, a later bed time, a special treat, extra time to play a favorite game, play outside with peers, or other incentives that your child finds desirable. Parent and child come up with a "price" for each incentive. For example, a total of ten chips can buy an extra fifteen minutes of TV before bed- time, or five chips can earn a cone of ice cream, while twenty-five chips will allow him to redeem them for a special trip to the zoo with his parents. The child may earn tokens (pick those that you want to use from the ones listed above or come up with your own) for positive behavior such as following directions, completing chores, and accepting responsibility. Parents and child should decide together what constitutes a desirable behavior and how much a child can earn in a given day.

It is best to be as specific as possible and implement the reward system on a consistent basis. Both parents should keep track of the child's progress by tracking it on a dry-erase board or a weekly calendar. You may want to allocate two days a week such as Tuesday and Saturday when the child will be able to redeem his tokens. It is best to designate a specific time☐after dinner or after chores are done☐and keep this time consistent. In addition, you may decide that five tokens will be the most a child can earn in a day. You can give the tokens out at the end of the day before bedtime to ensure that the child is motivated to do well throughout the day. If the child acts out, he does not earn a token until his behavior improves.

During the days of "purchasing" or "exchanging" tokens for privileges and/or incentives, the child may decide not to redeem his tokens but rather, to save them for a larger incentive. For example, if going to the zoo requires twenty tokens and he has earned only ten, it is up to him to use these tokens now or earn ten more. The larger the incentive, the more tokens may be earned. It is best to create the reward system with the age of the child and his abilities in mind. If the child misbehaves during the day, you as a parent may decide to withhold a token by explaining that due to his acting out, he was not able to earn a token that day. However, the parent will need to point out that the child will be eligible to earn tokens the following day and allow him child to see that positive choices lead to positive outcomes while poor choices result in negative ones. If the child had earned some tokens and this is the day to make a "purchase," but he is acting out inappropriately, the child should wait until the next day assigned for exchange of tokens to redeem them for an incentive. For example, you may have decided that tokens can be redeemed only on Tuesdays and Saturdays,

DON'T LOSE YOUR TEMPER

so if you have decided to allow him to redeem his earned tokens on Tuesday but he is misbehaving, you will then let him know that he will have to wait until Saturday to redeem his tokens. A very young or impulsive child may not be able to earn twenty-five or fifty tokens before redeeming them for a larger incentive in a given week. Thus parents should set smaller goals with shorter time frames and then increase them with time once the child is used to the rewards program.

For example, a younger or impulsive child may be able to earn ten tokens in a week and each five tokens may be redeemable for some kind of incentive, based on what he likes. A younger child may not be able to wait several days to redeem his tokens so, taking this under consideration, you may decide on what days he may redeem his tokens. Younger children may also be able to earn tokens for things like putting their clothes or toys away or going to bed without tantrums.

The Act Model as a Tool in Limit Setting

One easy and convenient way for parents to effectively set limits is to use the ACT Model, which stands for:

A — Acknowledge the child's feelings. Act immediately (avoid power struggles, over-reactions, and rescuing the child, or making excuses for not disciplining him).

C — Consequent appropriately (remain consistent; give out logical and age appropriate consequences; avoid scolding, blaming, punishing).

T — Treat the child sensibly and age appropriately (be fair, respectful, encouraging, and remain composed). Allow the child the opportunity to earn a privilege or, if he had lost parental trust, to be able to earn it back.

Now let us explore this in more detail:

Acknowledging the Child's Feelings

Behavior is driven by our needs and wants. Children, like adults, do whatever they need to do in order to obtain what they want. Therefore, if you as a parent, can determine what your child desires, you will have the opportunity to use this to reinforce desirable behavior and extinguish misbehavior. For example:

Johnny is five years old. Every morning, his parents have a difficult time in making him eat his breakfast. He will not eat his cereal and will put up a fight. However, Dad knows that Johnny loves Superman.

He would play with his Superman toy and would be glued to the TV whenever Superman is on. One morning, Dad tells Johnny, "I know how much you like Superman, but in order to grow up and be strong as him, you must eat your breakfast. Milk makes you grow and builds muscle, too." Then Dad puts Johnny's Superman toy on the table and continues eating his own breakfast. After some hesitation, Johnny starts to eat breakfast and eats it every morning from now on.

Johnny's dad knew that Johnny admires Superman and used this opportunity to his advantage. He did not plead with Johnny nor did he punish him for not eating his cereal. Instead, he subtly encouraged cooperation by acknowledging Johnny's admiration of Superman, which in return encourages Johnny to follow through and eat his breakfast.

Another example: Molly is six years old and this is her first day of school. She cries and does not want to get ready. Mom knows that Molly has been playing doctor with her dolls and has been saying that she wants to be a doctor when she grows up. Mom tells, her, "Molly, I know you want to be a doctor when you grow up. The only way to do so is to go to school and learn. Every doctor has gone to school, just like you are to go today. Would you like to pick out a nice outfit for your fist day of class?"

Soon Molly follows through and gets ready. Once in a while, when Molly gets discouraged about school, her mom reminds her of her wish to be a doctor when she grows up. In this scenario, Mom used Molly's desire to be like a gown up by allowing her to see that the choices that she makes right now will allow her to reach her future goals. She also empowered Molly by allowing her to choose her clothes for school that day.

Children are future adults who are taught by the adults in their lives. At times, all a child wants is to be heard. On some level, he understands that adults make and reinforce the rules in his life. When a child is frustrated, disappointed, or sad, he wants his feelings to be acknowledged in the same way as when his mom is upset if he does not do what she asked of him. With, children actions definitely speak louder than words because most of the time they will not say what they really feel. Most of the time, they will slam the door, cry, and throw a tantrum or fight with his siblings, hide his report card, or do anything that is indicative of his feelings.

The sensible parent will pick up on these external cues and will act out at that moment. The parent may ask the child what is wrong and then acknowledge the child's feelings. For example, imagine that your ten-year-old son asks to go outside to play after he has finished his chores. You decline and he says: "It's not fair," and storms out of the room. As a parent, you need to acknowledge his feelings and examine your own behavior. Have you been inflexible? Have you disregarded his feelings in the past? Or is he exaggerating? You may then go to him and say something like, "I understand you're angry, but it took you too long to do your chores and now it is dark outside. Perhaps you can try tomorrow."

It is a good idea to let the child know what is expected of him and what the outcome of each scenario will be. Remember to be consistent and follow through.

Depending on the situation, you may also say something like: "I see you're disappointed because I did promise you to go outside when you're done. Since you finished your chores half an hour early, now you may go outside for half an hour. I'll call you to come back when your time is up and expect you to return promptly before it gets dark outside."

Does your child act out mostly at home and is well behaved at school? If so, this is a cue that he is acting out at home for a reason. Perhaps he is trying to get your attention. Children who feel that they are competing for attention with a sibling or a new-born baby for his parents' attention may misbehave as a result. Attention is a strong motivator for children. At times, they are so desperate for it that it won't matter whether they receive positive or negative attention.

Children returning home from visiting their non-custodial parent may also act out. Perhaps he is doing so in order to test you to see if you will be consistent in your parenting. In cases where one parent possesses characteristics of the sensible parent and the other of the reactive parent, children will misbehave, especially after spending time with the reactive parent. Since one of the characteristics of the reactive parent is a "hands off" attitude, the child gets mixed messages when he is expected by the sensible parent to do chores or is given a consequence for his unacceptable behavior. This may confuse children as they may misinterpret the parent's intention. For instance, the child is confused as to why there are no chores when he visits Dad on the weekend, or perhaps why there is a bedtime at dad's house, when there is none at Mom's house. It is the parent's responsibility to discuss this with the ex-partner and also to explain to the child that there are rules to be followed. As a parent you may say something like, "I know you don't have to put your dishes away when visiting Mom, but since you live here, everyone needs to contribute." Or "I know there's no bed time at Dad's house, but you're there on the weekends and when you're here, you have school in the morning."

Try to give age-appropriate explanations and avoid blaming the other parent. After all, you're trying to be a role model and to teach the child that ultimately he is the one responsible for his own choices and subsequent behaviors. Try to see who owns the problem, you or the child. If the child owns the problem and he continues to act out, try to implement the ACT model when disciplining him.

Setting consequences is good, but they must be doable. Otherwise, the child will get discouraged and most likely you will not see an improvement in his behavior. Just imagine what would happen if you set an objective in your life as an adult and the consequence is such that you cannot follow through. You wouldn't even think of doing it in the first place, right? A child must know that he is able and capable of correcting his errors. Otherwise he will get the message that he must be perfect in order to be accepted. This may lead to low self-esteem, discouragement, and future acting-out behaviors due to frustration. When you set a limit with your child, he learns that rules are out there, not to be broken but to be followed, and that you mean business. The child then learns that he can correct his behavior when he is allowed and encouraged to do so.

Once the child has met the expectations of a consequence, parents will need to spend some time with him to process feelings and to find out what the child could have done differently in order to avoid future misbehavior.

Exercise Questions:

1. How can you make sure that you reinforce the limits you set?

2. How can you teach your child the power of choices?

3. Why are too strict expectations and rigid limits not a good idea?

4. How can you be sure that the consequences you give are age and situation appropriate?

Chapter 33:

Discipline vs. Punishment

The following are common scenarios of some parents punishing their child:

"Do as I say or you'll get a spanking."

"Be quiet or I'll smack you."

"If you bring home another F, I'll pull out the paddle."

"Say you're sorry, young man, or I'll have you scrub the bathroom with a toothbrush.

For many parents, a question that comes to mind when they hear the above statements is the use of punishment as a discipline method. Many parents, as well as schools, go even further by using corporal punishment as a way of "keeping a youngster in check." Research findings report that children who undergo corporal punishment may act out, exhibit low self-esteem, and display poor socialization and poor academic performance. Yet parents and school personnel continue to employ such practices as a way to discipline a child.

Children who suffer physical punishment may experience shame, guilt, and physical and emotional pain, just to name a few. Perhaps physical punishment is viewed as an effective discipline tool by many, but is it effective and psychologically safe in the long run? Children learn through encouragement and modeling. Wouldn't it be better if adults could teach and discipline children through non-violent means? Some parents believe that "a spanking" solves a problem by halting the child's undesirable behavior. Are children learning self-control because of some therapeutic effect of corporal punishment or are their behaviors driven by fear?

The Difference between Discipline and Punishment

There is a huge difference between discipline and punishment. When a parent gives a consequence as a means of discipline, he teaches the child responsibility. Punishment, on the other hand, leads to fear and resentment. Another difference is that during a consequence, the child has the opportunity to correct his behavior while he does not during punishment. Punishment is a one-way street. When a child is punished, he may feel shame, guilt, fear, and resentment. Punishment sends him the message that "You're wrong and now you'll pay!" Once a child is punished, he has not been given the opportunity to correct his behavior or learn other appropriate responses. In return, he may feel discouraged at even trying to behave in the future. If all he has to look forward to each time he errs is a negative outcome, then why try, he reasons?

When a parent wants to punish a child for an undesirable behavior by taking away something valuable , it is best to give the child a chance to earn his privileges back. A child who has lost a privilege is a discouraged child. He may not be motivated to correct his behavior if he cannot earn the privilege back. Allowing the child to see that he has the power to correct his behavior teaches him responsibility and allows him to see that good behaviors lead to positive outcomes while undesirable behaviors lead to consequences.

Some examples of parents' statements:

Parent: "When you turn this F to a B, I will treat you to Chucky Cheese."

Parent: "Stealing is wrong. You would not want someone to steal your things. I will confiscate your video game and give it back to you after you apologize to your friend for stealing."

Parent: I am not pleased that you did not clean up your room. You will not be able to watch TV this evening but may watch tomorrow after you clean your room up."

Reasonable vs. Unreasonable Consequences

Another problem that arises during parenting is when a parent gives a child a consequence that is out of proportion for the deed in question. Some examples are: Parent: "You didn't finish your dinner so you can't watch TV for the rest of the week."

Parent: "You got an F on your test and now I'll take away your bicycle for the semester."

Parent: "You lied to me so I can't let you play outside this week."

Parent: "You broke your dad's watch and now you'll have to cut grass all summer to make the money to pay him back."

Consequences must be given within a reasonable time frame. For instance, think about the owner of a puppy that makes a mess on the carpet and the owner then punishes the puppy seven hours later. Will this be effective in teaching it that it has done something unacceptable, and will it associate his earlier behavior with this later punishment? If you answered no, then you will realize that the same applies to when you set conscequences for bad habits that your children does. In order to discipline a child sensibly, a parent must know how and when to consequent misbehavior. Yelling at a child in a store or in front of his friends or threatening a child with punishment is extremely counterproductive.

The following are some unhealthy parents' responses:

☐ Parent: "You'll see when we get home . . ."

☐ Parent: "I'm taking your Game Boy right now and you won't see it for a long, long time, young man."

☐ Parent: "Eat your supper now or else."

☐ Will spanking a child somehow improve his school performance?

☐ Will washing a girl's mouth with soap when she says a bad word teach her why it is not acceptable to say such words?

☐ Will pulling a child's ear teach him not to talk out of turn?

☐ Will public humiliation teach responsibility?

☐ The answer is no!

Some parents stick to the old rule that if such behaviors were done to them as kids, then they must have been effective. This is incorrect. Doing what their parents did is what they are doing with their children now because they do not understand how harmful such behavior is to a child's self-esteem. Punishment is implemented when parents are unwilling to spend time parenting sensibly and resort instead to "quick fix" punishments.

When a child is punished, the message is I am no good, I can't do anything right, so why try at all? Even though kids do not like to be given consequences, in the long run, they learn that they can create desirable outcomes in their life by behaving well and that even if they make a mistake, it can always be corrected. Try to avoid scolding and or criticizing the child when he misbehaves. Criticism is not a healthy way of addressing the situation and will only cause him to feel angry and resentful. To retaliate, he may act out in the future as a way of defending himself because, most likely, he has felt not only angry but also discouraged. Instead, try to apply the ACT Model to guide you in your response in addressing the situation.

Practice

Use the following scenarios to determine appropriate ways to discipline the child:

Scenario 1

Five-year-old Molly starts to throw a tantrum when her parents tell her to put her toys away because it is time for dinner. How should they discipline her?

Scenario 2

Johnny, who is seven, is giving out his food to the family dog under the table. How should his parents consequent him?

Scenario 3

Tony, who is eleven years old, came home with a stolen game.

What should his parents do?

Scenario 4

Tyrice hid his report card from his mom. Once she finds out about it, how should she handle this?

Exercise Questions:

1. What is the difference between consequence and punishment?

2. Why isn't punishment a healthy choice of discipline?

3. Why do we need to find other ways of discipline rather than using corporal punishment?

4. What are the components of effective consequencing for undesirable behavior?

Chapter 34:

Be mindful

Mindfulness is a state of mind, or way of being, which cultivates an awareness of the present moment. 'Mindfulness' has gained popularity in recent times, along with meditation. It is an ancient practice found in a range of Eastern philosophies, including Yoga, Buddhism and Taoism.

Jon Kabat-Zinn, Professor of Medicine Emeritus and founding director of the Stress Reduction Clinic and the Center for Mindfulness in Medicine, Health Care, and Society at the University of Massachusetts Medical School, calls it 'the art of conscious living.' When we are mindful of another we are fully present to the extent that we notice the colour, specks, and light flickering in their eyes, from moment to moment. Mindfulness is the art of fully seeing, hearing, touching and connecting with this other person in this one, unique, never-experienced-before moment.

When we are mindful of our young children, we understand that they can't see over the kitchen bench, or they need assistance reaching for the tub on the top shelf in the fridge. When we are mindful we are 'tuned in'. We anticipate environmental threats and obstacles, and we sense how scary, active, smelly, noisy and unpredictable the large dog is through the eyes of our child. When we are mindful we feelour responses, the places in our bodies where we ache and twinge as we react to what we experience.

Being mindful in a relationship is about being conscious of the other person's right to express how they are. Being mindful may be remembering that it is a kindness to others to not impose your emotional state or social customs on them. For example, a friend with Asperger's Syndrome hates being hugged; it makes his skin crawl for hours after. Would you want someone to feel that way after an encounter with you?

When we are mindful we are 'in' every moment and we observe each moment as it occurs, we are in a state where we can choose our responses and be in our power.

Being mindful is not about always being in a happy Zen-like place. It also includes the painful or unpleasant moments. It is about noting 'what is' and staying conscious throughout.

When we are mindful of our older children we understand that there can be relationship tensions, situations at work, money problems and unaddressed addictions in the picture. When we are mindful we get the whole picture and accept that that is how it is and we love them anyway. Unconditionally. Which is why, in the first week of parent mentoring, new clients are given a notebook and the instruction to be still and observe what is going on and then record what 'incidents' happened and what feelings were involved.

There are always—and it is ALWAYS—huge insights. Often insights into what is not there. Many clients notice that what is missing is a palette of emotions. Many realize they are stuck in an emotional range that compromises just one or two emotions—usually guilt, resentment or irritation/anger. At this point there need be no attempt to change the way things are. Simply be still to observe the dynamic.

Be mindful and observe your son or daughter and find out who they really are.

Be mindful and observe what your behavior may be saying about you.

Be mindful of what triggers you and your reactions.

Chapter 35:

Manage your mind

Look at these example scenarios;

My daughter and I were climbing along some rocks near the sea when we came across a ledge, covered with slippery leaves, above a steep drop. The two boys hopped across and turned to their younger sister, 'Careful Brittany.' The ledge was narrow but in my opinion not dangerous at all but Brittany faltered. I told her to step across; she looked uncertain and fearful.

'You can do it Brittany,' I said. 'What are you telling yourself?'

'I'm going to fall,' she said.

'Exactly! What about if you said to yourself I am balanced, I'm walking safely across?'

'I'll get across.'

Brittany safely stepped across.

Changing our focus involves switching our awareness from the outside to the inside. Brittany focused on the gap and the possible fall outside herself then focused on her awareness inside.

In a similar fashion, we can focus on what our kids are doing and choose to view it in a positive or negative light. Or in no light at all; we can stay neutral and simply observe what happens and focus on our own neutrality. After a certain age and point of maturity our kids are free to make their own decisions. It is their life (as they often like to tell us) and it is they who will live with the consequences.

Let's say your teenager 'borrows' your car without your permission and crashes it. How we now choose to see our child is up to us. We can focus on them being an untrustworthy thief or we can focus on other more positive things they are capable of--he's a go-getter, adventurous, a risk-taker. It's all about managing your perception.

If we stay neutral we may see this as a learning opportunity for our child, and us. After not learning smaller lessons about honoring other people's property and asking permission, our teenager has just had to learn this lesson in a bigger, more costly, more noticeable way.

We are in control of our minds and we have at our disposal the ability to choose our thoughts. We also have the power of imagination. Imagination will carry you; it shifts you from where you are to where you could be. No matter how bad we feel things are we have the power to envision and to see a new possibility. We can envision the future we want to create.

A single mother was frustrated with her son's sense of entitlement. He would lose his shoes at school and expect replacement ones. He would borrow money and not repay her. He had no close adult male role models.

When I asked her if she had talked with him about how he imagined his life as a grown-up she said she hadn't. Together we worked on a short script about what it meant to be a man. This is a portion of what she talked about with him:

A man pays people back, keeps his word, protects others, pays taxes and works hard. He doesn't give in or run away or fights. He has dignity. Self-worth. Self-respect. Compassion. Generosity. Humility.

The son did not change his ways immediately but this exercise made her feel better. She felt lighter and freer as she had fulfilled what she saw as her obligation to tell this boy what society would expect of him.

Even if you are in the pits of despair, what's the point of worrying? Instead, use your imagination to create a better reality or, at the very least, a more enjoyable fantasy!

Chapter 36:

Acceptance

Is there a child like one of these in your family?

☐ The child with no friends who just hangs around, doing nothing.

☐ The girl who wears too much makeup, short shorts and acts skanky.

☐ The sisters who lie and steal and will always deny it.

☐ The child who always gets into a fight.

☐ The girl who blames everyone else for everything that doesn't go her way.

☐ The boy who answers back, swears, and gets physically abusive.

☐ The child with the 'wrong' friends who wants to go out all night and will run away if you tell him he can't go.

These are all common scenarios that cause loving, caring parents so much grief because even though you may try to avoid identifying with your child, somehow or other your child's problem fighting becomes your fight. Your kids' social life becomes your social life. Your teen's skanky clothing choices becomes your poor taste.

No wonder we pass judgment. No wonder kids like this make us cross. No wonder we want to change them but we can't! The reality is your child is doing X and you are feeling Y. To heal the conflict and upsets between you and your child you need to accept the way things are. Stated more strongly: You cannot move into healing until you have accepted the way things are.

The question to consider is: how can you accept the way things are when every cell in your body is screaming that what you are seeing is unacceptable? How do you really, truly, deeply accept something? Do you accept something by going on a shopping binge, eating cake, having another drink? The best way I know to experience acceptance is to simply sit with it. It may be useful to remember that whatever you find hard to accept, someone, somewhere else in the world is dealing with far worse.

When we don't want to accept something, it is tempting to find something 'to do' to distract us, or some other thing for us to think about. But then, while we are thinking about that something else, we are not doing the business of accepting whatever it is we find hard to accept.

I know of no better way to find acceptance than to sit and let the feelings, thoughts, and waves of emotions percolate, wash, and radiate through us. Until finally there is a shift to acceptance. True acceptance is a state in which you no longer respond to the triggers that used to cause a reaction in you. It is a state in which you co-exist with the way things are and can see the situation how it really is, and not through emotional filters.

Have you identified any issues you fight as a parent? I, for example, used to think my children 'should' be bright and polite, early in the morning—that was what was expected of me when I was a child. I used to think they 'should' have the self-control to manage their moods and remain civil and I felt constantly offended when they were rude and I would feel as though I had 'failed' as a parent to teach them to be nicer.

YET, the fact is I was always surly in the morning and my parents never succeeded in getting me to arise all sunshine and smiles. I mastered this art when I was a mother, in my thirties, expecting my kids to do better than me. When I accepted this truth I altered my expectations and went with it. People awake grumpy in the morning and I now accept that. They're not going to stay that way all day and I get off to a less stressful start.

Another expectation we may have is the ideal of a perfect family. Really? Where on earth did that idea come from? It may not be as romantic an idea but the truth is—to be a parent means to experience conflict.

A friend was upset when his son turned down the opportunity to be a pilot choosing to 'throw it all away' to live in a foreign country with a young woman he had just met. This friend had always wanted to be a pilot but had failed the vision test. It took years for him to accept his son's decision and for the heartache to subside. I might think he could have accepted this reality sooner but this was his process.

As an outsider it is easy to see the dynamic but when we are in it ourselves we are so attached to all our values, hopes, expectations and dreams. What we deem 'acceptable' and 'unacceptable' are simply opinions. As we cling to our ideas of what is right or wrong in 'our book' we forget that our child's life is 'their book'.

Parenting demands personal growth—and it's often not what we thought we had signed up for when we chose to have a child. The sooner we truly, deeply reach the state of acceptance the sooner we can resolve conflict, harmonize and move on.

Conclusion

Whether you're a parent puzzled about your child's anger and temperament, or one whoe's going through a major life change like divorce and want to be prepared to tackle your child's reactions, I hope the insights in this book benefited you personally. Here are some pointers to take with you:

Anger is an important part of life

Accept your child's anger and help him channel it to constructive ends. Help your child understand that feeling angry is normal but acting violently when angry can have negative consequences. Unearth the story of your child's pain. Without this uncovering, anger can pile up for many years. Fixing the cause usually tames the anger.

Model appropriate expressions of anger

Remember, your child learns from your example. Don't expose your child to conflicts between you and his other parent. Kids can develop resentment and bitterness in their lives as a result of parental conflict.

Know yourself and your child

This knowledge enables you to choose a more effective and sensitive response when confronted with your child's temper. Your child is his own person. Understand that his temperament and personality are part of the unique qualities that make him special. Don't deny him a healthy self-esteem by expecting him to meet your preconceived notions of who he should be.

Be patient

Learning to channel anger in healthy ways takes time. In fact, many adults haven't mastered managing their anger either.

Be there to show affection

Kids are usually calmed by their parents' presence and warmth.

When you understand the nature of anger and deal with your angry child equipped with this understanding, you are improving his chance of living a happy and successful life. After all, just like happy emotions, unpleasant feelings of anger are vital in helping every one of us make sense of life's complexity and evaluate our experiences.

Did You Like Don't Lose Your Temper?

Before you go, we'd like to say "thank you" for purchasing our book. So a big thanks for downloading this book and reading all the way to the end. Now we'd like ask for a *small* favour. Could you please take a minute or two and leave a review for this book on Amazon

This feedback will help us continue writing this kind of books. And if you loved it, then please let me know.

Leave a review for this book on Amazon by searching for the title,

Don't Lose Your Temper

Want to read more exciting stories for FREE?

Join my **V.I.P** List now!

I regularly GIVEAWAY FREE books and SPECIAL DISCOUNTS!

Join my mailing list and be one of thousands we already receiving FREEBIES!

Join by visiting this site:

paulseidel@ravenspress.com

Or Scan this QR Code from your smartphone to go the website directly

21481119R00070

Printed in Great Britain
by Amazon